A Life Like Mine

A Life Like Mine

◆

A Remarkable True Reflection of a Family's Inspiring Emigration Story

E. L. Baird

iUniverse, Inc.
New York Bloomington Shanghai

A Life Like Mine
A Remarkable True Reflection of a Family's Inspiring Emigration Story

iUniverse books may be ordered through booksellers or by contacting:

iUniverse
1663 Liberty Drive
Bloomington, IN 47403
www.iuniverse.com
1-800-Authors (1-800-288-4677)

ISBN: 978-0-595-48513-0 (pbk)
ISBN: 978-0-595-48883-4 (cloth)
ISBN: 978-0-595-60605-4 (ebk)

Printed in the United States of America

Contents

Acknowledgements

I would like to dedicate this book to my loving husband Lance, if it was not for his hard work and true dedication this dream would never have come true, thank you darling.

To my three children Laura, Elijah and Joshua for being so patient and for understanding that Mum is busy! And for the big hugs.

To all of my family and friends for their support over the years. With love and many thankyou's.

Introduction

The word emigration conjures up all sorts of different thoughts and images in people from all walks of life, to some emigration brings the feeling of loneliness, isolation, fear and even betrayal either to king and country or to the nearest and dearest family and friends. These feelings are totally understandable, we all have family and friends and the security of our home country, the country where we were born and grew into our very own individual identities, a country where we feel safe.

However in the ever-changing world of politics, social change and varying economy some have lost that warm snug homely security blanket, loss of homeland identity, so they yearn for a more comfortable easier to fit into version. For those people emigration means fresh hope and new ideas. Everyday life brings a new meaning with great excitement; the waking up in the morning where everyday will hold new surprises and inspirations. I know the feeling well. A dream that will one day become reality after the hours and hours of thinking, reading, researching and of course the relentless phone calls and e-mails. Those clear visions of a dream life to be played out in another country inside that big world of ours.

Thousands of people each year leave behind their family and friends and jobs to pack up and leave their home country in search for that brighter, happier more fulfilled life, a clean slate.

In the UK emigration has increased, in 2001 53,000 people emigrated and in 2006 that figure had doubled with 107,000 people leaving for a new life, that is roughly 2000 people a week. Can you believe it? I am sure that in the next two years this data will again have increased enormously. So why are so many people leaving? A question we all think we have answers to but in fact they are purely ideas, reasoning's to what is going wrong, our own personal thoughts and opinions. It is a question that we cannot directly answer in our changing society; the answer to the question is an open debate, a debate that will continue for some time. So along with those opinions we leave.

All I can say is there is nothing better than watching your family grow and thrive without restraints, without the worry of how they will cope in the future, to be able to see them prosper into caring, intellectual individuals where a good job and a nice house does not mean a long chain of debt hanging around their neck. With that in mind it does not appear that emigration is such a challenge and on many a pair of lips is the question "If so many thousands are doing it then it can't be that hard can it?" My answer is simply "Yes, it is very hard, in fact sometimes the emigration process seems an impossible feat" The ideas are easy, the decisions and carrying them out can be a hard puzzle. I have likened it to a hurdle race, it looks easy at the beginning but once you start running and hitting those hurdles it gets quite tough, in fact some of those hurdles are so tall a very long ladder is required to get over them!

However in order to settle successfully in a new country with a new government, new rules and regulations and a whole new way of doing things requires a certain amount of grit and determination mixed with a large helping of "a jolly good sense of humour" I have to say that this is definitely on the essential criteria list.

I have written this book in order to share our experiences of emigration both positive and negative through the eyes of my family. The book is aimed to bring to the general audience a true-life family memoir that should be enjoyed by all readers. I relate to our experiences in New Zealand and Canada up to the date of book completion although our story will continue!

Since August 2005 my family and I have moved to two different countries, from the United Kingdom to New Zealand and from New Zealand to Canada. We have experienced first hand a good deal of the red tape that is associated with a move out of your home country, such as finding work, new school rules and the buying and selling of houses along with a whole heap of other new things that must be dealt with. I do not hold any academic qualifications in moving from country to country but the wealth of information I have gained through the different stages of our moves has provided me with the knowledge suitable to write about our experiences with confidence and detail.

A Life Like Mine is not an emigration help manual as such; it is a family memoir that relates to our own emigration journey. Although I have included some information relating to the emigration procedure the information in the book is based on our own experience at the time.

The book is written in the order in which the events happened, including our excursions that form part of our whole emigration experience. These extra holiday excursions have been included in the book in order to provide the whole story. It is important to me that the reader gets the whole picture of our time travelling.

I also feel that it is important that you the reader have a small picture of us before commencing to read the main part of the book. Therefore the next section is a brief introduction of my family members.

My Family

Well hello from us all, we are a family of five, pretty normal I think, well I shall leave that one up to you as you may have other ideas about us once you have finished reading the book!

Let's start with me; I am Emma, main author of the book. I am a pretty chilled out sort of lady, don't stress out too much, and take everything in my stride. Well most days anyway, there is the odd off day! I grew up on a farm located in North Wales, up near the Denbigh Moors, a great life with plenty of fresh air, animals and freedom, being able to find a quiet spot to think and reflect on life at that time. When I was eighteen I left the comfort of the farm and settled in the small town of Denbigh, where in 1995 my eldest son was born.

In 2000 I met Lance and within three years we had two lovely children. We were married in November 2004. Lance is the bread and butter earner so he has the hardest job or so he says! Seriously though this whole experience would not have been possible without him and his career. Lance is a Laboratory Scientist, an occupation that is in short demand in New Zealand, Canada and a few other countries so it could be said that the world is truly our oyster.

Some of you may be familiar with the Skilled Shortage Occupations in the countries mentioned and will realise that if you or your partners occupation is listed in those categories then the immigration process is ready and waiting for you, if you are not familiar with the Skilled Shortage Lists don't worry I will explain in further detail later on in the book.

Lance had a similar upbringing to mine on a small holding not too far away, in a small village near Ruthin. They had a few animals to tend and a lovely Welsh farmhouse surrounded by beautiful countryside. I have been told that he and his pals would get up to all sorts of tricks and they did or so I have been told!

Then there is Laura, Laura is very much like her mum, an animal lover especially of horses and given the opportunity she would live with a good menagerie of animals. She has a good imagination with plenty of creativeness and she is a good story-teller.

My youngest son Elijah is a boy full of testosterone, levels above his age I am sure! He is a rough and tumble boy into all things boyish, Spiderman being the greatest at this moment in time. He does have a gentle loving side and cares greatly about his siblings, he looks out for his older brother and sister in and around the home. It has to be said that Elijah appears older than his four years.

Joshua is my eldest son and is from my first marriage of which I shall not go into. Joshua has a different nature than his siblings, he is shy and quiet, not really interested in too much rough and tumble. He enjoys reading and the quieter activities in life. Well that is my family so now to the important part. As with all good things the hardest part is the beginning so we had better start there, Enjoy!

The Start

Our real inspiring emigration thoughts came about after Laura was born in 2001, it had been a topic of brief conversation prior to Laura's arrival but these first talks were fruitless and quickly forgotten, lost in the usual mix of everyday events.

We had been lucky enough to buy our three bedroom semi-detached house in Denbigh in 2001 before the big property boom in the UK occurred so our life was relatively comfortable. Lance worked as a Laboratory Scientist in the local general hospital and I worked as a Support worker in a residential college for people with learning difficulties. We had our family and friends within close distance and saw them all regularly.

Like many people in the UK we enjoyed watching the emigration shows on television, seeing people daringly move to another country, some would succeed and for others it would all end in disaster. For those readers who are not familiar with these emigration shows they are a short account of the emigration stories undertaken by others and shown on TV. Watching these shows became a sort of routine for us, to make sure we were in to watch these programmes and after a time we would go onto the Internet in a quest to try to find out about these people to see how they faired after the show. It was really a good down hill spiral for us!

We then started to look at different Internet sites and even different countries, however Canada stood out time and time again but at that time it was purely out of interest as we had made no firm decision. Lance continued to work at the hospital and I at the college.

In August 2001 Laura was born and that was the turning point for us, having another child had changed our thoughts on life in the UK and we realised from the time spent on the Internet that there were places out there where we could have a much better life. Along with Laura our emigration dream was born, the question then was where?

Canada was always our main interest although I have to say here that Lance would have happily gone to Australia, however I am admittedly scared of most things small and hairy well to be totally honest scared of most things small that crawl and creep! My vision of Australia was not the beautiful scenery, clear blue seas and white beaches but rather a country where I would be faced daily with deadly nasties lurking around every corner. Not to mention the fact that Australia has the highest population of deadliest creatures on the planet, no not for me!

Whether it was a coincidence or in our heads I do not know but Lance and I both started to feel a slight air of doom and gloom over our life, maybe it was the thought of a better life elsewhere putting our current life at that time into a room with a dim light bulb!

Lance started to become increasingly unhappy and frustrated at work, he felt trapped with little option for career progression. It did not help when the laboratory manager retired and was replaced with a less well tolerant person, very hard to approach. The five years at the hospital seemed to becoming a life sentence for him.

Changes for the worst were also becoming a regular occurrence at my place of work, instead of enjoying going to work I ended up dreading it which meant the whole day leading up to my evening shift was totally ruined beyond belief. The only way to see the light at the end of the tunnel was to hit the Internet hard of an evening and research. We were very lucky in respect that Canada was our only real choice so it made it a slightly easier process to gain the information needed, too much information about more than one country can easily lead to mix ups and confusion. It is wise to research one country at a time rather than them all at once and keep all information separated in a file. It is easy to scramble you're brains with one country's rules/regulations and requirements without dealing with half a dozen!

The period between Laura's arrival in 2001 and Elijah's birth in July 2003 was generally spent purely researching Canada and its different provinces and its huge expanse. Canada's population in 2006 was 31,612,897 people compared with the UK's population in 2006 of around 59,209,500, however it is easy to see and quite unbelievable based on total land area of these two countries that the United Kingdom is far more populated with the UK's total land area standing at 244,110 sq km's comparing that to Canada's enormous total land area of 9,017,698 sq km's. We do have to bear in mind though that a reasonable portion of Canada is sparsely populated due to the harsh climate.

It maybe hard to believe but it took us from 2001 to 2003 to find general information about Canada, obviously the regular internet sessions were cut down due to the three children, it also gave the computer a rest. I am sure it would have given up the ghost at some point with the constant on and off.

In early 2003 we came across a website which mentioned an annual emigration seminar that was held each year at Sandown

Racecourse in Esher, Surrey, UK. It was the biggest emigration seminar of its kind and a must go for all people interested in or actually going through the emigration process. We booked our tickets that were not all that cheap, booked our train tickets that were also not that cheap and booked the babysitter (my parents) who were thankfully free! How exiting it was going to be, information city, talks and plenty of companies to meet who could offer us advice, even the Canadian Immigration was to be there. Two whole floors of pure emigration indulgence, not all Canada of course, France and other European countries, New Zealand, Australia and America where the other places.

So the big day arrived, my parents turned up bleary eyed at 5am in the morning, our train was at 6am so early start all round. We could not wait to arrive at Esher and hit the stalls! From memory the trip took around 3 hours and I can remember saying to Lance "I wonder how many other people are going to the emigration fair, they will all be on the way to work"

Eventually we arrived and got off the train, the racecourse is actually visible from the train station so off we trotted along the road towards our destination. After a while it became clear that we had actually gone completely the wrong way so in fear of missing all the talks we had to hastily turn around and go the other way at a very brisk pace. Well after a good fifteen-minute hike we found the right place and entered red faced but still full of anticipation of what it would be all about.

What I am about to write is the honest truth; it was the biggest waste of time and money ever, for us anyway. We could have held some of the talks, we could have stood on those stands and offered advice as it became very quickly apparent that our long period of research had indeed left us as experienced as some of the professionals there. We learnt nothing and to top it off my father phoned to tell us that Laura was quite poorly, subsequently she had a febrile convulsion that very night due to a fever and ear infection.

After our Esher disaster we collaborated all our information and sat down to decide what our next step would be, it has to be said that the only next step was either to forget the whole thing or indeed apply for permanent residence in Canada and that is exactly what we started to do. All the information and forms required are available to download on the Canadian Immigration website which is of course listed at the back of this book. The information provided below is the information that we used to guide us through the Canadian Residence application process back in 2004 when we submitted our application. The information is subject to change at any time and should not be taken as legal advice. It should also be remembered for those of you who wish to emigrate that all applications could vary due to individual circumstances.

Federal Skilled Worker Category
This category is for those who have a good level of education usually a higher qualification such as a degree and a job that is portable to Canada, a job that is skilled and that will help Canada's economy and employment gaps. There is also a Provincial Nominee Program in which you can apply directly to your chosen province. That particular province will then look at your application, if you have been nominated by an employer then they will send you a Provincial Nominee certificate which you will then send with a separate application to Citizenship and Immigration Canada (CIC). Unlike those who apply under the Federal Skilled Workers Category the Provincial Nominee Program does not require you to be assessed on the six selection factors.

Business Category's (Investors, Entrepreneurs and the Self-Employed)
The first two categories here require good business knowledge and a certain amount of money to bring into Canada or Net Worth depending on the category chosen. The self-employed option requires the applicant to have experience relative to their occupation and that they have the intention, experience and ability to start a business or operate a farm successfully in Canada.

Family Class
Those people who are over 18 and are either Canadian citizens or permanent residents of Canada can sponsor close family members who want to become permanent residents of Canada.

It is a requirement that you undergo a full medical examination and have chest x-rays carried out (the x-rays are required for all over the age of 11). These must be undertaken with a designated professional listed on the Immigration website and must not be undertaken until the Immigration Department have asked that you have them done.

The applicant pays for the medicals; x-rays and blood tests so it is advisable to phone a few practitioners in your area as they can vary considerably in price and some do charge an administration fee.

NOC (National Occupation Classification)
The NOC is a classification system for all jobs in Canada, in order to be eligible to apply for permanent residence under the Federal Skilled Workers class an occupation must be listed as Skill Type O or Skill level A or B plus experi-

ence in that occupation for at least a year in the last ten years is required. It all sounds very confusing but it really isn't, believe me! Have a look at the NOC occupation list that is located on the Canadian Immigration website. Find the appropriate occupation and there will be a four digit code next to it, this is the code that is needed to put on one of the immigration forms. For example a Registered Nurse's NOC number is 3152.

The Six-Selection Factors—
When applying under the Federal Skilled Workers Category (not the Provincial Nominee Programme) an application will be determined on six factors, this works on each factor having a number of points to be gained.
Education—25 points
Ability in French/English—24 points
Experience—21 points
Age—10 points
Arranged Employment—10
Adaptability—10

There is a maximum of 100 points that can be gained; however the pass mark in 2004 was 67 points. If we would have had less than 67 points we would have not been eligible to apply for permanent residence in Canada at that time.

There are other categories in which permanent residence can be applied for, however I have only briefly covered the main three. For further information on all the categories' visit the Canadian Immigration Website, this will provide all the information you need and of course you will be able to download and print the required information relevant to your situation.

The best advice I can give is to thoroughly research the countries that interest you, try to avoid some of the Immigration agents sites as they have generally a one-way street and are not all that honest in presenting the bad points of a country, some of these companies make money out of the inexperienced who do not know any different and telling you the not so good things is not in their best interest. However there are some very good genuine companies out there who can offer you a great wealth of advice so look hard. I have listed a few at the back of the book for your convenience. We found that looking at the countries government websites helped, as they know what is happening in their country, obviously I am stating the obvious here! They have many links that will take you to what you need to know.

We therefore set about downloading and printing all the forms and there was quite a few! At that point we realised just how much work we had to do even before we could send the application in. The information required on the forms was just unbelievable and we really did think that some of it would just be impossible to obtain especially the part where we had to recall what we had been doing for the past ten years. I struggle to remember what I was doing this time last week so my grey matter was in for a serious work out.

Once we got over the initial shock of all that lay on the table in front of us we arranged the documents in plastic sleeves, it is easier to tackle a large amount of paperwork if it is in relative order rather than being all over the place.

The first area that we started with was to make a list of the information that was required from other places, university, past and present employers. At that stage I asked all family members including stepparents and step or half brothers/sisters what their birth dates and addresses were in order to get them right. We had to fill in a section that required all of that information so it had to be accurate.

It is the waiting on others that takes time, especially a university that your husband left six years ago. The forms asked us for the most in depth details about our family, although the bulk of the information is only relevant to the adults in the family and those children/adolescents over 16 years of age.

It is important to take time over the questions as rushing will lead to extra mistakes being made which in turn makes the whole thing extra frustrating and of course takes extra time. Lance is not too keen on his writing style and worried that the Canadian Immigration would not be able to read any of the forms! So I was responsible for all the writing and completion of each and every form but that was fine I did not mind.

I discovered that it was a good idea to actually write all the information down on a note pad first and fill in at least two practice forms, doing that enabled me to triple check everything was correct before attempting to fill in the forms that would eventually be sent.

Loose bits of A4 were pointless as they just went astray, never to be seen again. I lost several pieces of paper with important information on.

I know it may sound really over the top to fill in a couple of practice forms, it truly helped, however I did have to undertake more than one attempt at the "to be sent forms" as it was so easy to get carried away and put a wrong digit in the date of birth section or make a spelling error, there was nothing else for it then but to start a new form all over again.

A large quantity of printer ink was essential as we used it, but the most important thing was to scan and save every single form that we completed perfectly. If the application was successful we knew that we would be asked for updated information and that meant repeating some of the same details that was on our original application forms so keeping copies was important. Would you be able to remember all of those personal details on all of those forms from that far back? Unfortunately we did not scan and save all of our forms, we do not know why but when we got the updated information forms late in 2006 we had to do most of them from memory, we knew very well that some of the information we gave at that point would not correspond exactly with the information on our original application.

The Canadian High Commission is extremely thorough, any mistakes or conflicting information on the forms can lead to an application being refused. The basic rule was to copy everything, a rule we did not adhere to. A time did come when we needed to refer to those forms again and we did not have copies of some of them. It included all the immigration forms, letters from educational institutions and employment history/references.

We spent lots of time filling in paperwork and contacting people, the immigration forms would not be completed in two weeks unless our contacts and ourselves were super human. People had their own very busy work schedules and they could not have been expected to drop everything to complete a letter or find details that we needed to precede with our application. Patience was important, as getting frustrated would only lead to there being further delays on purpose on their behalf, there is a difference between friendly reminders and constant harassment!

From downloading our forms to the actual residence application being sent to the Canadian High Commission on the 4th November 2004 was roughly about eight months.

One of the worst times in the whole overall emigration process is the first week or two after the application has been sent. We had spent months and months working on something for sometimes hours and hours a day, it became our life, our project and almost a personal vice. People can require hours of therapy to successfully give up a vice such as smoking, it is true to say that those first few weeks were spent twiddling thumbs, feeling bored and trying to search for something to do. It is a natural response to stop doing something that has taken up such a big part of your life. There is also an air of worry in case that precious package goes missing on route or it gets damaged somehow, unlikely if it is sent by a reliable door to door courier service but imaginations have a tendency to run away when one is under stress. It was just under two weeks before we had a little brown envelope pop through the letterbox with the Canadian High Commission stamp on it, inside was a simple card, a confirmation receipt that they had received our application.

Our research prior to completing our application involved finding out roughly how long the process of immigration to Canada can actually take from application submission to receiving your actual permanent residence and being able to leave your homeland. It became apparent that it could indeed take some time but less than two years was at that time a rough idea. Both of us knew that deep down but again optimistic human nature had our application done and dusted within a few months. Although we knew the true timescale in the back of our heads where we tried to keep it you can imagine our shock when that little card stated "You may not hear from us for at least twenty one months" We had worked so hard for this and to wait at least twenty one months before even hearing anything about our application was quite frankly sole destroying!

I have to say that when the Canadian High Commission state you will not hear anything they mean it, a point, which I shall no doubt refer back to later in the book along with the fact that they are almost totally un-contactable.

We had little choice but to resign ourselves to the fact that we would be living in the UK (North Wales) for quite a while longer, that we would not be leaving our quite frankly awful jobs and Laura and Josh would continue to attend a school in the UK. It was a real bitter pill to swallow! We tried very hard to make it work and stay happy and focused on life in Denbigh but despite our best efforts in the end it was an uphill struggle, we just could not do it, it was not in our planned itinerary.

There comes a point in time when all dreams and realisations meet head to head and some very hard decisions have to be made, we had reached that point and we were determined to find a solution.

That solution would wait a little longer whilst we busily planned the forthcoming Canadian holiday, we were going to tour the Rockies in a motor home for the whole month of June. The holiday was approaching fast and we had a route to plan and holiday stuff to buy. We are the sort of people that can manage quite easily to arrange more than one important matter in our lives at any one time so along with the impending holiday we set about looking for that get out of the UK clause that we could not put off any longer despite a very good effort to do so. By the time we were due to fly out to Canada we had indeed found a solution and had arranged the most important aspects of it.

We had thrown ourselves into the whole emigration thing without truly realising or thinking at all what we would do after our application had gone, we had pulled the wool over our own eyes with relation to timescale and was not at all prepared for the hard hitting fact that we would not be emigrating to Canada for at least two years. There is a very good saying "Time flies" and it is a true saying, time does fly by but at the beginning of a two-year period that you didn't bargain on the time flying seems an awful long way off.

Although I do have to admit, once we had found our solution time moved very fast, I think that was due to the fact that we had found something else to get our teeth into, something to brighten up our lives once again. The feeling of hope had completely overtaken the feeling of despair; the Baird family was back with a vengeance and our family and friends were about to hear a big announcement, a surprise that they had least expected. We had decided to move, and not within the UK!

Holiday Time

We arrived at the Calgary International Airport on the 2nd June 2005 and were enthusiastically greeted by the many volunteers that work at the airport; they provide general advice and a ride on a golf cart from the arrivals lounge if you need it.

We were so exited to be in Canada as many people can only ever dream about going on holiday to such a nice destination. I know many of my work colleagues were rather green at the news of our holiday.

We had booked a night in the airport hotel as it was a requirement by the motor home company that we do that rather than driving a big vehicle immediately after a long flight, it made sense as you are most definitely not at your best to take on board all the information needed to have an enjoyable trip.

The hotel room was adequate, a bit on the small side but manageable. We ordered an in room meal which was delicious and the children received a free glass of warm milk and a cookie each, a nice touch to the end of a busy day. The next morning we went for a small dip in the indoor pool which was free for guests and it was not long before the smell of cooked bacon and sausage could not be resisted any longer and the buffet breakfast beckoned our rumbling stomachs. We ate like we had never eaten before as it was not that cheap and we made sure we got our money's worth.

Time was going by and we were ready to hitch a taxi ride to the motor home company in Calgary. When the holiday was booked we decided on a twenty-four foot motor home, it was big enough for a family of five, however admittedly we were both very nervous about the prospect of driving it! It was also the first time that we would have driven on the other side of the road; it was all a bit of a concern. So you can imagine our shock and horror when we arrived at the motor home company to hear that we had in fact been allocated a motor home four foot longer than we had booked, a twenty-eight foot one for no extra charge of course. We did not know why but we presume it was an oversight on their behalf, an oversight that at the time did not land at all well.

After the safety talk and vehicle introduction we set off to navigate our way out of Calgary in order to start our Canadian adventure after many weeks of anticipation. Lance could not get to grips with driving such a large vehicle; automatics were new to us so I took over the driving, as we would have not gone anywhere otherwise. I did not mind too much although getting out of Calgary was pretty stressful at times as the main highway was extremely busy.

We soon hit the open road and headed for our first night in the Canadian wilderness at Banff. Driving the motor home was actually quite easy on the open road and with no gears to fluff it was plain sailing once we reached cruising speed on the Highway.

It was not too long before we got our first glimpse of the Rocky Mountains and just as we had imagined them to be they were stunning. We had also come across some rough weather that hampered our progress but that was all part and parcel of the experience I suppose.

We had collected some good road maps before our holiday started and as usual we went too far, way past the sign for Banff and our campsite, I blamed the poor road signs but it was our mistake. We turned around at the earliest opportunity and headed back to the site, the campsite was located next to the Hoodoos, a spectacular formation of stone standing tall all in a row, and they are quite magnificent.

Once we had hooked the motor home up to the power and water outlet outside we double-checked it was done correctly, the last thing we needed on the very first night was to break something important. After double checking everything we felt happy that our first effort was good enough so we all set out for a short walk around the campsite before retiring to the motor home for the evening to talk about bears and all things Canadian.

We hit the road the next morning and headed into the town of Banff but we did not realise that the roads were going to be so tight and we decided that until we were used to the twenty eight foot vehicle we were driving it was best to stay clear of small roads with tight turnings. We therefore made our way slowly towards Jasper taking in all the beautiful scenery along the way.

Our next two nights were spent at the same campsite near Lake Louise, a very nice wooded campsite situated next to a beautiful ice blue river.

We were advised to try and book each campsite the day before or to at least turn up at a chosen site if we had one in mind in the morning when people are leaving to almost guarantee a space. Campsites get full very quickly from mid afternoon onwards so we had to plan a day ahead if it was possible to do so.

It is a requirement in Canada that all campers, tents and motor homes spend each night at a campsite rather than just pulling up in any lay by for the evening. Obviously there are some rather nasty animals in Canada and the last thing we needed was to be out toileting at night half asleep and fall on top of a grizzly! Those rules are there to protect you and the Canadian wildlife, not to be difficult. At times it was awfully tempting to stop for the night at some of the nice secluded road stops but common sense always prevailed.

The weather had been wet since we had entered the Rockies but it did not dampen our enthusiasm to explore the campsite. With raincoats on and with Elijah in his buggy off we went for a nice walk along the rivers edge, through the forest. We had not gone too far when we noticed a red sign attached to a tree warning that a grizzly bear had been seen in the campsite a few days prior. Now at that point we started to feel rather uncomfortable and extremely worried, so the best thing to do was to turn around. It was at that point that we noticed that one of the log cabins at the campsite had most of it's veranda ripped to bits so it did not take too long to put two and two together and come up with four! Hastily we returned to the main road of the campsite and rather than wander into unknown territory we stuck to the road and walked feeling less under threat to the wildlife centre and a small selection of shops.

Once back inside the motor home we sat down and looked through the guides and attractions leaflets that we had picked up in the visitors centre in order to plan the next day. We had purchased a newspaper in the shop and was horrified to read on the first page that a well known runner from Canmore, which is just down the road from Lake Louise had been out running and had surprised a grizzly bear, sadly with fatal consequences. It really made us think of the real dangers that lived in the forests. Although bear attacks are very rare in Canada there is always that chance of an encounter if you spend time in their habitat. We had to be aware and take precautions, not walking into obvious bear places such as thick forest and keeping to clearly marked paths. Those who frequently walk in bear country have a bear bell attached to their bag or clothing, these bells are designed to alert any bears in the area that you are coming and that it is time for them to move on, bear bells save many hikers lives each year and a very good simple invention.

We decided on the route for the next day, tucked the children up in their beds and sat and enjoyed a glass or two of wine.

Unfortunately we had chosen a spot next to a hidden railway track that during the daytime was not that noticeable. As soon as the site quietened at around ten o'clock we had regular trains going past. In addition with the pelting rain on the roof we were in for a rough nights sleep and that is exactly what we got!

The next morning was met with fuzzy heads so the first thing on the agenda was to arrange with the wardens a different spot for the second night, a more secluded quieter spot on the campsite hopefully train free.

With a new site number designated and after drinking a few cups of extra-strength coffee and a bowl of cereal for breakfast, we headed off for our days excursions. First stop was Lake Louise and despite the damp weather it was picturesque just like all the photographs you see in magazines and on the holiday television programmes. The lake was a wonderful colour of turquoise like many in the Canadian Rockies. We later found out that the colour is from the silt particles washed down in the glacial water that reflect the light. It is such a beautiful place with the soaring mountains as a backdrop. The only disappointment was the building work that was being carried out at the time on the hotel, it made the place look somewhat untidy but I suppose with the amount of tourists that visit Canada each year there is bound to be a call for further development.

There is plenty to see around the Lake Louise area including a rather long uphill journey to Moraine Lake, when I say a long uphill journey I mean it, it was very steep and admittedly I was not too keen on driving our huge motor home up it or down it! However it was a slight comfort when we arrived at the top to see that many other motor homes had also made it up the hill and some were even bigger than ours.

The lake itself was again beautiful although not as impressive as Lake Louise but nonetheless it had its own charm. There was a very strange very large pile of rocks next to the lake and it was very hard to come up with a solution to how they got to be there, I suppose it was one of those phenomenons that cannot easily be explained. It was still raining but we did decide to have a stroll up past the pile of rocks where a hiking path had been established, I was not convinced about it being an established route but more like a narrow track. We were also well aware of the sign at the bottom of the track informing hikers that a mum grizzly with young lived nearby. We had had enough of a scare at the campsite so we managed to walk a few steps up the track until we turned a corner and could not see the bottom anymore so that was our queue to turn around and go back. We descended the rather precarious looking road back to our campsite and that took around twenty minutes give or take a few.

It may not appear that we spent much time out that day but with food and drink stops plus taking the many photograph opportunities that there are in that area the day soon goes by.

The new camp spot that we had chosen for our last night at that site was much better despite it being more in grizzly bear territory but we did not intend to go creeping around in silly places or wandering in the forest at night. No we would remain in the comfort of our house on wheels for the evening where we felt much safer.

The next day we carried on up Highway 93, the Ice Fields Parkway, that particular route is supposed to be the most scenic route in the Rockies and I have to say at that time I could not really see why but it must have that label for a reason, maybe it is spectacular in the snow.

We took a small detour into British Columbia along Highway 1, the Kicking Horse Pass and followed a winding road to Emerald Lake. Along that road we also stopped at a few waterfalls that were worth seeing. It is surprising how many places there are off the main roads and it pays well to divert onto them.

Emerald Lake was indeed very well named, the colour was just un-imaginable, and it was beautiful. It is totally amazing how a body of water can look like that. It was a quaint little place with holiday cottages over looking the pristine glass like lake, the only disturbance on the surface were the plentiful fish catching the flies, trout we presumed. It was probably one of the most beautiful remote off the beaten track places I have ever seen to this day; it truly was a magical place that I can still picture very clearly.

We drove a little way into Yoho National Park before turning around to meet the 93 North again and continue our drive towards Jasper that was still some kilometres away. It is hard to believe unless you have been along that route how many lakes and waterfalls there are along that stretch of road. It was obvious now what they meant by the most scenic highway in the Rockies. Not the actual road like I thought but the stunning diverse scenery we were seeing and it was not long before we were in awe again.

I explained earlier why some of the lakes had a turquoise colour, Lake Peyto was something else and to the children's delight there was snow on the path to the lookout platform. Peyto Lake was quite a distance below and away from the platform, slightly in the distance but close enough to see the many different colours in the water again from the glacial silt reflecting the light. We had read that moose and elk and even the odd bear could sometimes be seen drinking but there was no wildlife that day. However we were not disappointed and enjoyed the short walk back to our home, especially the sliding in the snow part!

There is such an abundance of things to see along that highway that we just could not do it all. We did see the Columbia Ice Field though that had featured in many a movie and been on many holiday programmes. The shoulder season as it is known is the time when Spring is turning to Summer and the glacier certainly did not look at it's best and not what we expected but you cannot expect everything to be perfect.

The scenery around that area called the Sunwapta Pass was a dramatic change from complete greenery to a desolate almost slate appearance. It was another example of how quickly the landscape could change and how steep some of the roads could get. It was bleak but not in such a bad way, there were some great lookout spots and it was all part of the wonderful place.

It was also the start of Jasper National Park that covers a huge expanse; a place we had heard was full of Canadian wildlife. That was the place to see the moose, the wolves, the bears and all the other large animals that we hoped to see.

It was not too long before the bleakness turned once more into the lush green grass and forest we were used to. The nice thing was the little gaps in between the trees, little glades of flowers that you could imagine yourselves sitting in and having a lovely picnic. Those little areas that were totally out of bounds and soon it became apparent why it would have been a very bad idea to set out your cake and sandwiches on a blanket.

We noticed a car had stopped on the side of the road and the lady passenger was pointing towards the trees with three fingers, we had no idea what was going on until we suddenly saw three Black Bears grazing on the sweet grass and flowers in one of the glades. They were the most gorgeous animals, not phased by us at all and they even crossed the road right in front of the motor home making sure they stopped and looked in each direction to make sure it was safe to cross. We must have watched those three bears for fifteen minutes before they slowly entered the forest and out of sight. What a great start to Jasper it was, we could not have been luckier.

Time was getting on and we knew we still had a fair way to go before reaching our campsite at Jasper but we still stopped at Athabasca Falls on the way. It was black bear country, easily recognisable from the rubbish bins; there are two different types of metal bin, those to deter the grizzly (large) and those to deter the blacks (medium). The falls themselves were nice but we were now really pushing for time and it was one of those moments when we really were tempted to camp there in the car park until a ranger turned up and we knew that the area was obviously well patrolled. There was nothing else for it, we had to hit the road and fast if we were going to make it to the camp or we would have really been spending a night in the great outdoors. Luck was on our side that evening as we made good time, I think our rumbling tummies played a small part in us reaching our destination with some to time to spare.

We were just in time as the campsite was very busy, plenty of people queuing at the ticket offices for spaces and we were fortunate that there was a site available although it was not powered. That was fine with us, as we had stayed at a powered site the previous couple of nights so the motor home was well stocked up with water and the battery charged sufficiently to see to our needs throughout the evening and into the next morning. It was a nice treed site with plenty of room between the campers so you felt that there was some amount of privacy to be had.

The local female Elk were calving in the campsite and a notice near the entrance warned that they could be aggressive, so it was advised to steer clear if you saw one nearby. How exiting it would be to witness a newborn elk.

We drove around looking for a suitable area as that campsite let us choose our spot within the camp and that was a nice touch. After a couple of circuits around and seeing some elk we eventually settled on a nice secluded treed area and with my help Lance backed our motor home into its space.

It was time to settle the hunger pangs before taking a walk around the camp; it was a lovely evening so why not?

After our meal we went through the usual routine of covering ourselves with mosquito repellent and tucking our clothes in, mosquitos are extremely clever and will bite you in places you would never have thought they could get to so it is important to protect everyone well. It had come to our attention on the initial drive around that there was a small playground near by so we thought it would be a nice idea for the children to have a good play before bed. We had all spent quite a few hours that day sat in our seats so we were all feeling in need of some exercise especially Laura and Elijah who by then were chomping at the bit even though Elijah was strapped into his buggy! Off we headed in the direction of the playground and after only walking a few meters we noticed an elk in a clearing between the trees. She was not too close and busy eating so we did not pay her any attention and carried on past. It was almost instantly that I noticed that although we were not paying her any attention she had certainly been watching us all walk by and more worrying was the fact that she was leisurely following us. We all decided to speed up a bit and walk a little faster to get away from her but she had other ideas and she increased her pace in our direction. The situation was quickly turning into a bad nightmare as the hackles on her tail were well and truly up, she meant business as we had stepped into her domain and she was not at all happy. Instinct made us run but unfortunately I was pushing Elijah in the pushchair and could not go as quickly as Lance, Laura and Josh who were in front of me plus trying to push a buggy over a forest floor is not too easy. All the time I was watching over my shoulder and I could plainly see that she was also running and quickly gaining on me. I had little option other than to stop, turn around and confront her head on. By now Lance had reached a small building and to his dismay it was locked, there was nowhere to run or hide. I quickly placed Elijah in his buggy behind me as there was no way she was going to get him, it really was a mother against a mother and that angry elk was no more than a meter away from me. She was enormous much bigger than a Red Deer and they are not small. Adrenalin and the pure motherly instinct of protecting the child behind me was the only driving force keeping me from turning tail and surely enduring a full on attack from her. Elk kill more people in Canada than bears, a thought I was well aware of at that time. It was a stand off situation, she was not to keen on having a head to head battle and neither was I but I could not be defeated and take my gaze and dominant stance away. Thankfully she started to back up despite her stamping hooves and snorting in protest that I found very intimidating indeed. To my relief Lance had come to my rescue like a knight in shining armour. After making sure the children were in no danger, he ripped up a broken tree stump from the ground and rushed towards the elk with a you back off or else approach. It worked; the elk backed away and slowly walked off back to her patch. We had won the battle. I can say I have never felt so threatened by any animal before and we were all shaken by the event, apart from little Elijah who was too young to know how much danger he was in.

With shaking limbs we went back to the motor home to recover and to put the children into bed. Once the children were settled we sat outside the camper with a bottle of wine reflecting on our close shave. It was not long before we heard a very distressed lady shouting for help. That same elk had decided to attack someone else. In fact she attempted an attack on four other campers that evening and was clearly not happy with all the people around. She was extremely dangerous.

As dark was falling we were lucky to witness two park rangers carry a small new born elk onto the road near our camper and under their instruction to be quiet we watched them lure the angry mummy elk away with the help of her crying calf and they were both safely removed from the campsite. She just could not stay there when she could have so easily seriously hurt or even killed someone.

We had all indeed got our wish of seeing some Canadian wildlife close up, too close up it has be said. We most certainly got more than we had bargained for and as you will read later in the book it was not to be the first time we were to have a very close shave with another famous Canadian creature.

The following day we had just about recovered from the elk ordeal, booked a second night at the camp and was preparing for the day that lay ahead, a day that would be hopefully less of a challenge.

We set off from camp reasonably early, as we wanted to see quite a few sights that day if all went well and we did not have any more bad encounters of the animal kind.

Jasper town was as expected, small and quaint but sadly it had become very commercialised and that spoilt the original character that I am sure still lurked under the surface. With the food and drinks cupboard re-stocked we drove slowly towards Maligne Lake, the roads on that route were nice and straight so the driver could also enjoy the scenery to a certain degree and look out for those all important photograph opportunities. There was not too much wildlife to be seen although we did see a Coyote looking rather sheepish on the side of the highway.

After a couple of kilometres we turned off the main highway and onto the road that would lead us to Maligne Lake. The road was busy in both directions and as we drove past Medicine Lake that I have to say was also very beautiful surrounded by its rock structures the traffic in front of us slowed down and stopped rather abruptly. We could not see any reason for the hold up apart from maybe the leading coach had run into engine trouble but after a few minutes the coach speeded up and went on its way. A kilometre or so later the coach came to a halt again so it was rather a mystery to what was going on with it. It was only when the coach started to move that the problem became clear. A lone Mountain Sheep had been in front of the coach on the road all that way! It had been walking and running in front of the coach without veering off onto the grass verge. Silly animal but it was so funny to see the expression on its face as we drove past. A real expression of annoyance and almost an air of arrogance was written all over that sheep's face, it was definitely worth a picture for the album.

It was about another forty five-minute drive to Maligne Lake past many other pretty little lakes with no name. They were plentiful around that area and worth a quick stop to see if we could see anything moving around the waters edge. As it appeared on the map the road does finish at Maligne Lake, it just comes to a dead end and turns into forest.

The first thing we noticed as we were getting out of the camper was the amount of mosquitoes around so plenty of repellent was needed. I just do not know what it is but I could be wearing a protective suit smeared in bottles of repellent and the mozzies would still get me. The rest of the family have learned just to stand near me and they will be fine! With a full dose of repellent on and with Lance, Laura and Elijah at close quarters we walked across the bridge that would take us to the waters edge.

There was an unbelievable sight in the river and an anglers dream. As we are keen anglers we wished that we had brought our fishing rods as the river was literally teeming with salmon and trout. It was one of those moments when we both felt that really desperate need to fish. It was such a carrot in front of the donkey moment but we could do little and besides even if we did have rods we probably could not have fished there, maybe the fish knew that they were safe and so they just swam plainly in view teasing us.

The Lake is famous for the little island in the middle that you can canoe to or hire a boat if you so wish. Hiring one is the only real way to see the island close up as it is quite a distance from the shore but we were getting seriously harassed by mosquitoes and at that time a boat ride with that army did not appeal in any way so we settled for some long distance photographs and a look in the shop.

On the return journey heading back towards the 93 we noticed that there were five or six cars parked up on the side of the road near Medicine Lake and as they all had there hazard lights on we knew that there must have been something in the area. We pulled our camper onto the verge and found that the attraction was a big male black bear grazing in the dry riverbed, the dry riverbed that we had walked on an hour or so earlier! It was entirely possible that the bear could have been watching us but that was just a general assumption on our behalf. We got out of the camper for a better look and to take some photographs along with the hoards of other people trying to get that magic shot. However the sighting was short lived as a huge coach came roaring around the corner and the bear ran for cover into his forest.

We had been in Canada for less than a week and we had seen four black bears. Some people can spend months on end in Canada and never see a thing so we felt very privileged indeed to have seen them.

Once we reached the main road that led to Jasper and our campsite we thought we would turn right instead of left and we headed towards a place called Pocahontas and Miette Hot

Springs. The route takes you along Jasper Lake and we captured some extremely nice photographs along the way. The lake is very long and is on both sides of the road, with the mountains reflection visible in the still water that creates a lovely picture.

The road to Miette Hot Springs was not the best road we had been on it was very twisty and steep in places and rather narrow but we persevered onwards regardless of the terrain, as we knew that it would be worth all the effort. We drove for what seemed like hours but finally arrived at the Springs and after paying at the kiosk and of course putting our swimming gear on we entered the hot mineral water and it was hot, after only a few minutes I had to sit on the edge. I have to highly recommend Miette Hot Springs; it really was well worth the long drive to get to it. The location is beautiful with a view of the mountains and surrounding forests. At the time we were there the car park was a playground for a herd of wild sheep so there was also some entertainment to watch whilst we soaked. I have to tell you and it is very important that if you do ever venture there please remember to take a good pair of sunglasses and a hat into the pool with you as the sun is blinding. We did not and even after just ten minutes our eyes were sore due to the brightness and the constant squinting. Half an hour of baking was plenty for us so a nice cold drink and a slice of cake finished of with a couple of warm berry muffins with cream were in order. After our not so healthy feast we made our way back to camp, it was unfortunate as on the way back we passed a lovely secluded campsite at Pocahontas but we had booked another night at Elks Ville so we carried on slightly disappointed in the fact we had already paid to stay somewhere else.

The second night at the camp was calm and quiet with no wild elk terrorising the campers. We certainly had more than enough excitement the previous day that we had not bargained for so it was a nice change to be able to sit outside without constantly being on high alert and looking over our shoulders every few minutes for a pouncing elk.

Our Alberta tour had come to end for now as we made our way across to British Columbia. The scenery changed quite quickly from the thick dense forest to more useable land and it appeared from first impressions that BC was a very different province with the high annual rainfall noticeable at once!

Our accommodation was not booked for that night so it was a case of see what we could find on route.

Blue River was the first place we came across that had a couple of campsites so Blue River it would be that night. The first camp we went to was ridiculously tight for such a big vehicle so we decided against it. Just navigating out of the place was a nightmare with the trees being so close together but my good driving skills got us out!

Before our holiday we had looked on the Internet for campsites and one we did like was also in Blue River so it was there that we went. It has to be said that people in the tourism industry cannot have a dishonest website, as common sense would tell you it is obviously bad for business. That campground host had not quite got the grasp of that concept as we found out upon arrival. On the website the campsite was a lovely well kept site but the real clincher was the brightly coloured authentic tepees that you could hire to sleep in, a real novel theme considering the Native Indian history of Canada. So you can imagine the excitement of the children when we found that particular campsite, if the photographs on the website were anything to go by then it should have been great fun for all of us. You may have already guessed, the campsite was a run down shack of a place and the tepees were just a few sticks tied together with a few pieces of mouldy material. Either the pictures on the Internet were well out of date or the owner had a very good designer, either way it was not a good place. There were quiet a few horror movies out at that time that usually depicted a family or a group of people losing their way and ending up in a down beat freaky place. A freaky place that is full of cannibals that drive around in the night in big old trucks picking them off one by one. In our opinion that campsite was a prime spot for such a movie and with darkness falling we had little choice in staying in our motor home hoping that the evening would go by quick. With bolted doors and windows we slept not so well with the nice thought of ending up in a cooking pot alongside some potatoes and carrots!

In order not to bore you I will skip a few days here as to be honest there was not a great deal to tell you about the places we visited over those next few days.

From the Blue River film set we travelled onwards towards our main destination of Revelstoke but before that we passed through the city of Kamloops. Kamloops was a very different place and the scenery was quite bleak in my opinion. It did not seem to belong in Canada but rather more suited in Spain or Greece, a very desolate arid landscape where even the buildings looked out of place.

It was here that we saw our first big Wal-Mart and as Asda (a big UK supermarket chain) is owned by Wal-Mart we thought it would be good place to food shop and stock up on essentials, we were to be disappointed. Unlike Asda it did not have much of a grocery selection and what they did have was not really what we wanted but we had to buy a few items just to keep us going until we found a better supermarket. After a quick supermarket sweep we went to the till to pay for the items in our trolley.

That is when our little Elijah decided to throw the biggest tantrum he has ever had! He had been quite happy pushing the trolley around the supermarket but as soon as it came to a halt at the till and he could not push it anymore he made a fuss. In fact he made such a fuss that no amount of reasoning was to help so the only solution was to remove him from the store and with a very red face that is exactly what I did. Elijah screamed so much the whole store could hear him and he refused to walk so it was a case of dragging him across the car park as every time I picked him up he just hit and kicked me. Eventually I managed to get him to the motor home still kicking and screaming. The attention of passers by was great and it was not surprising as his screams sounded awful but after an agonising five minutes he calmed down and we set off.

I am sure it was due to stress and not liking the big city of Kamloops much but we forgot to get fuel so it was lucky that we came across a small garage just down the highway and reached it just in time I am sure.

Our intentions were to stay at a campsite/horse ranch somewhere off the beaten track near Kamloops that on the initial directions given seemed relatively easy to find. Common sense did not prevail at that moment when it should have but in our defence we were not equipped with hindsight either. Finding the place proved difficult and after twenty minutes of driving into the middle of nowhere we decided to flag a lone car down and ask for further directions. According to the occupants of the car we were right on top of the place so we continued for at least a further ten minutes, all the time the road taking us more into the middle of no mans land and further away from the main road. The road was bad and up and down all over the place, the fuel economy was not good and it was already getting low by that point. The only option was to turn back and look for another less remote camp for the night. On the way back we missed our turning and the road started to look very unfamiliar, time to ask for directions again! We pulled over and Lance walked to a nearby house and regretted it as soon as he knocked on the door, the place itself was very run down and he noticed that the man and the children did not have shoes, they were obviously very poor and not well educated. For those readers who may take offence at that please don't as it is not meant to offend the less well-off people. The point I am trying to get across is the feeling of being an alien in an unknown wilderness, totally lost and low on fuel with my husband talking to a family that looked rather odd. Lance had also taken note that the family car and indeed the front porch of their shack was completely bashed in with huge claw marks, marks only a Grizzly Bear could have made. The man pointed us in the right direction and we hurried back to the main highway and what a relief it was to see that again, we had started to get worried!

I was back to the map regarding a camp for the night and so we continued along the road passed Little Shuswap Lake and Shuswap Lake, the larger twin, we could not find the campsites there either and it was getting late, we were getting tired due to the distance we had driven that day and the children were hungry and starting to moan.

The biggest issue was not that we could not find a single place to stay but we had not topped the fuel up on reaching the highway and on entering Salmon Arm the red light came on indicating low fuel, it was a very worrying few minutes. Thankfully with no time to spare we came to a hill that we coasted down to a very welcome garage at the bottom of it where we filled up the motor home with some well-needed fuel. It was at the garage that we managed to arrange our night's camp at a site a few miles down the road. It was not the best, the owner was a grumpy old man, the weather had turned horrible but we had at least been saved from a night on the side of the road.

Despite the pouring rain and the flies Lance and I sat outside with our raincoats on and had a few well-deserved beers whilst finally seeing the funny side of our eventful day that was not the first or the last.

The next two days were to be much better and with more excitement of the animal kind. Revelstoke was the next stop and it was not to disappoint us in anyway shape or form from the moment we arrived. We had seen many pictures of Revelstoke on the Internet during our holiday plans and we knew to expect a wonderfully picturesque place.

Our first taste of Revelstoke was to come in the form of a small Wild Strawberry and driving off the beaten track here actually paid off for us as we noticed a chap picking something on the side of the road, we stopped to ask what he was foraging for. The whole area was covered in dainty strawberries, sweet juicy little things and after asking the gentleman if it was ok to pick some we did. In fact we picked bowls full of them not to mention the fact that we had a fair belly full at the same time. The children were in their element and with big smiles and red faces they picked and picked and ate and ate. The strawberries grew there every year due to the good soil and the guy went each year to pick them and to make jam with the berries he could not eat quick enough, the rich bounty was enough for the locals and also a welcome variation to the local bears diet. After picking more than our fair share we headed back into Revelstoke to find our campsite, the campsite was chosen well in advance for a couple of reasons, the location and for us the fishing lake.

The campsite was under new management and they had done the place up well, I can honestly say it was one of the nicest camps we stayed at during our holiday and a spot we would go back to in the future.

Mount Revelstoke with its snowy peak was plainly visible through the trees, the only downfall was the weather, it had been wet most of the time and the forecast was not too good for the following couple of days.

Our spirits would not be dampened and we made sure that we would enjoy the site and the lake even if we did not catch a single thing.

Our first night was spent inside as the rain did come down heavy but that was fine and a nice change from the previous days rush.

The next day was a brighter sunnier day and we had a look around the town and sampled the local cookies before returning to the site for a fish and for the children to have a play on the playground. The rain re-appeared and Lance took the children back to the motor home whilst I had another half an hour's fish catching nothing and not having a bite. Boredom soon set in and I returned fishless for the lovely dinner Lance had specially prepared for us all. Looking back I am glad really that I went back when I did as not having a bite may have turned into a different meaning altogether as close calls with Canadian wildlife were not too welcome after Mrs Elk in Jasper.

With tea finished and a nice fire lit outside we tucked the children into their beds and sat outside warming our hands on the fire, it was drizzling but not enough to force us inside as the air was fresh and welcoming. It was then a car pulled up and asked if we had any young children, strange we thought, but we answered by saying that the children were tucked up in bed. The question was not at all strange once we had been informed that an unknown rogue black bear was wandering around the campsite at that time and that unaccompanied small children could be in danger. It was not too long before we noticed several campers walking over towards the lake where I had been fishing less than an hour before to observe the bear. It was a young black bear and it had found the tent near the lakes edge interesting to say the least.

A few of us were actually getting quite concerned about the poor person in that tent that had no idea of the possible dangerous situation that they could have been in or had any idea that a bear was a few feet away from them. It turned out later that the person in the tent had been eating fish and chips inside so we all understood what had caught the bear's attention and the reason for it hanging around for as long as it did. It was amazing to watch a wild animal in such close proximity to humans but on the other side of the coin sad to think that it is those bears that can be very dangerous to us and likely to become problem bears leading them inevitably to be relocated or even destroyed. The bear was mesmerizing to all who watched and even the possible danger did not stop those with cameras and video cameras taking those extra steps toward the bear for the better shots, we were just as guilty of that as most. After a period of maybe half an hour of sniffing around the tent the bear moved away towards the main camp building, toilets, washrooms and garbage bins. This is were we noticed that the new owners had not put steel bear bins in and the reason why the bear had visited. It was an unknown bear but that did not mean it had not been at that camp before, easily accessible bins meant easy food for a hungry young bear. The power of the animal was plain to see as it shook the bins trying to gain a meal, it really brought it home that if a black bear was so powerful at half the size what could a grizzly be capable of.

Darkness was falling and visibility was poor, the bear had lost interest in the bins and moved off heading for the row of motor homes that ours was a part of! My intuition knew that we had to get back to the motor home then, as I knew that bear was heading in that direction and neither Lance nor I wanted to bump into it at the front door. I am being truthful here, we walked to the front door and went inside, I went to the back window and the bear was outside looking around and smelling our now gone out fire for morsels that may have been cooked. I am convinced that the bear was on the other side of the motor home before we even arrived, our timing was impeccable, an extra few minutes stood around could have proved a few minutes too long. It is very unlikely for an adolescent bear to attack a fully-grown adult although the risk of an attack should never be dismissed. That bear had not fully grown but was big enough to have caused serious harm or death if it was extremely hungry and intent on a big meal.

Revelstoke had provided us with the fifth black bear of our holiday, we had been blessed in the bear department and as many people told us some who have lived in Canada and in the United States might have never even seen one and we had seen five in just one month, unbelievable. Leaving that place was hard I can tell you but as we had a deadline to meet we had to tear ourselves away and carry on with our trip. We did travel as far as we could up Mount Revelstoke and captured some lovely images, both of the native flora and fauna and of the magnificent views of Revelstoke town and beyond from a high vantage point. Lake Balsam, a small lake located at the summit was particularly picturesque with its snowy edges and mirror reflections of the forest. After the excitement of Revelstoke with its bear and strawberries the rest of British Columbia appeared less entertaining.

It is just a fact of life that all places in the world in every country will have its own good and the not so good spots. The two have to come together to build a true picture of a place, nowhere is perfect but at times that is hard to remember.

Rogers Pass with it disappearing glacier was next and the local gang of gopher's that resided in the lay-by added some cute entertainment by eating crackers from out of our hands. They were well acclimatised to the two-legged species feeding them and they were not at all scared of humans. After the photographs were taken and we had enjoyed a hot cup of coffee we continued along Highway 95. After passing through the Glacier National Park and the British Columbia Glacier National Park we headed south towards the border. There was little chance in making the trip to the Canadian/American border in one day and to be honest despite thinking of trying we did not. We had slightly fallen behind schedule and we were concerned that if we did not make good headway in the next few days that were to follow we would have to abandon the plan to enter America and visit Idaho and Montana. That was a plan we had set from the start and we did not want to give up on it, however it would be a good few days of gaining some kilometres back on the clock if we were to complete our itinerary on time.

Despite having the behind schedule issue in our mind we could not resist stopping at a campsite just outside Radium as we had heard that the hot mineral springs there were very well worth a visit.

At the local campsite we had another moment with the motor home but in our defence it was the campsite owners fault and not ours. We paid the tariff for the night and made our way to the allocated spot and could not quite understand how we were expected to fit a twenty-eight foot motor home into it. The space was totally inadequate and on quite a slope, you may have figured out by now that I will not be defeated with regards to difficult parking and after some shimmying about I parked the motor home in a pretty perfect position all be it on an angle! It was perfect parking to me. Lance was less than impressed with the spot and went back to the office to ask for another location, it was funny but the lady was just about to come and tell us to go to another pitch as she had not seen the size of the motor home when we drove in. She could not believe that we had actually managed to get into the spot but we moved anyway to a better larger area.

The following morning we visited the springs and they were nice but unlike Miette they smelt strongly of sulphur and the water was extremely hot so after about half an hour we felt rather frazzled and had soaked enough so after showers and a drink to re-hydrate we departed Radium to continue our travels.

The scenery became quite flat from that point and the Rockies slowly vanished into the distance along with the heavy forested areas and that was rather sad to us, we had loved seeing that sort of scenery but Cranbrook beckoned and we had to go.

By the time we reached Cranbrook we had both been driving for quite a few hours and really could not face anymore so we thought it would be a good idea to stay the night and make our way to the American border the next day after some well needed rest. It was not to be as the campsite in Cranbrook was just not our cup of tea so we continued on and eventually came across a provincial campground, Moyie Lake Provincial Park Campground. It was a true wilderness campsite with plenty of spots to pick from and of course it had the added bonus of the lake for fishing. In fact it was one of the best places to go if you wanted to be eaten alive by mosquitoes, they were in huge numbers and very keen on fresh food!

I can say that I was so happy that the windows in the motor home were equipped with insect netting, as we would have literally been sucked dry. The heat from the food cooking was like a huge signal to them to come in droves and they sat on the mesh waiting, of course there was no way that they could have got in through that.

The ranger, a Chinese chap, came along to collect the park fee and within minutes he was covered in mosquitoes, from head to toe, it was in a way funny to see but I am sure he did not think it was amusing in the least to have an extra pair of living clothes on. It was quite understandable that he did not want to hang around making conversation with us, as he probably needed to cover himself in bite relief cream and have a good itch!

After having a good chuckle over the poor ravaged ranger we put coats on and took the children for a brief play at the playground, brief due to the huge thunder storm that had developed within about ten minutes of us all getting out of the door. The rain was torrential for a good half an hour but it soon cleared up afterwards so we lit a campfire in the pit provided. The idea behind the fire was to frighten the mosquitoes away when we went to sit out to have a few glasses of Canadian whisky once the children were in bed.

To this day I still cannot fathom why we sat outside on plastic bags to stop our posteriors getting wet with our trousers tucked into our socks and our rain coat hoods tied tight around our necks. The whisky must have thinned the notion that we were protected from the super stubborn mosquitoes that plagued us. They were that invasive that even with a citronella candle lit and our clothes smothered in mosquito repellent they still came for their supper. It has to be said that we looked rather peculiar and we do have photographic evidence to prove it!

The next day the ranger was not the only one itching and scratching at the numerous bites we had received during our brain numbing session outside. It was an experience that we will remember for sure and an experience we hope not to repeat any time in the future.

It was time to head across the border into America and our concern over the patrolling American officers was in a way well justified. The officers were to the point in the questions they asked; mainly did we have firearms, any alcohol or dangerous citrus fruit. Luckily we had drunk the majority of the alcohol the previous night and the small amount we had was not a problem, our cupboards were not full of oranges and lemons so no problem there either. They asked us to park up and go into the office to get our Green Cards and that gave one officer the opportunity to search the motor home briefly. Of course we were not harbouring anything that would bring criminal charges but I suppose they had to check. The whole time in that office was absolutely nerve racking for us both, we felt like criminals despite the somewhat forced friendly manner of the officer dealing with our Green Cards. It was hard to concentrate on his idle chit chat when we were too well aware of the gun protection the officers carried plus the true fact that at any moment they might have to use them. It was not a comfortable time at all and not a good place for the children although they did not have a clue what it was all about and the potential situation of a mad gunman trying to cross the border either way. The officer took what seemed ages to complete our Green Cards and put them carefully into our passports. Once they were done and he was satisfied we were genuine we were ushered on our way and welcomed into the United States of America.

Idaho and Montana

We were so relieved to have crossed the border into America in one piece. The whole process was so worrying but we had arrived and it was a great feeling to be able to explore a very small proportion of the American countryside.

At that point in time we had made some good headway on our schedule but we knew that we could not hang around too much in America so a sort of whistle stop tour was all we could have hoped for. That being said though it was better than not seeing America at all and that could have been a serious possibility if we had not knuckled down to some serious driving! Driving at first was merely a crawl; we could not believe that they drove so slow in America. As soon as we crossed over the border into America we had to slow down to thirty kph, much slower than we were used to driving in Canada! In fact we were going so slow the native snails were passing us by and after a few kilometres we were thinking we might have to break the speed limit in order to actually get anywhere. The problem was and what nobody had bothered to tell us was in Canada distance is measured in kilometres but in America it changes to miles, it all became very clear; we had been travelling at thirty kph instead of thirty mph! As you will know there is a considerable difference between the two but once we had realised and adjusted our speed we moved along more swiftly and caught up with those snails.

We had already planned where we were to stay for our first night in Idaho, a campsite where the two rivers, the Moyie and the Kootenai merged.

The campsite was not too far into Idaho and the first true place that we believed we would catch some fish. We had become used to the lack of fresh fish in our diet and it would make a tasty change to have a good trout or two in the frying pan.

The journey down the steep muddy track to the campsite was scary, there were no places to pull over if you met another vehicle coming up so we just crossed everything and hoped we would not. Reversing up a steep hill was not at all a good idea in a twenty-eight foot vehicle.

Once we had settled into our space we thought we would get the fishing rods out and go and see what, if anything, we would catch. The first cast on my part was not bad and landed in a still pool away from the turbulent swells and within a fraction of a second of the bait sinking and the float settling on the surface a rather large fish had taken the bait and was heading down stream at a fair rate of knots! At that point I did not know what species of fish it was but I was pretty certain it was not a trout, trout fight and despite the fish taking some line it soon became tired and I managed to gain the line back on the reel. The fish came into the shallow waters slowly but surely and we could see that it was a large fish but like I had guessed no trout. A fish supper was well needed so after a bang on the head we took the unknown fish back to be prepared for tea. It turned out that the fish was full of tiny pin bones and every mouthful contained more bones than flesh so after a few agonising chews and plenty of water to wash it down we gave up. We found out afterwards that the fish were not seen as a good eating fish due to the many bones and that they were known as Whitefish, not the whitefish species that we are more familiar with in the UK that are good eating such as haddock or cod. The eating quality of the fish was no good but some of them were large and provided good sport for us with their willingness to eat the bait we provided on our hooks.

On a completely different subject most people I am sure go away on holiday to get away from the usual daily routine. Not the couple that were a few rows away from us, they had the most superior motor home, you know the big ones that are bus shaped and cost an arm and a leg. Well they spent the whole time we were there watching their outside television set most of the time. They never moved, only to go to the toilet or to eat and drink which I am sure was done whilst they were watching TV, the eating and drinking part I mean! It was quite bizarre in our eyes to go away on holiday and spend the whole time glued to the TV getting serious square eye syndrome. I suppose that there are many reasons behind such strange behaviour and I should not criticise those who undertake non-stop television watching as their main holiday activity, let them be I say.

The campsite was so peaceful and we decided to stay a second night and instead of the second day spent mostly fishing we tried our hands at the crazy golf course that went down well with the children and a couple of rounds did not break the bank.

It was time to leave Idaho after our brief fleeting visit and cross into Montana the next state along.

It was our very first stop in a small town called Troy in Montana that led to our continued wish to go back to that area and at the time of writing we still yearn to go back.

There is the most wonderful, picturesque, fabulous place in Montana past Troy called Libby and I ask that all who read this book should at some point in their life visit that place. Libby Dam further up from the town is a paradise on its own merit and for all who enjoy natural beauty, freedom camping and the great outdoors it is a must. It was at Libby that we had one of the most memorable times out of the whole month we were away and we will never have that opinion changed. We had seen the majestic Rockies, visited all the big well known places but none were in our eyes as good as Libby, an unknown marvel.

As soon as we drove up to the recreation area we knew that we would be spending more than one day there. The dam was home to a couple of bald eagles, wonderful birds with a good talent for aerial acrobatics and they were not afraid to show their talents off to us. The water itself was completely clear and by the numerous people fishing it was obviously a good fishing spot. That place was just perfect and for once we had some real sunshine to bask in rather than rain to soak in.

It was not too long before our fishing bug surfaced again and we had to go and give it a go, the slight downfall was the route to the water was down some treacherous rocks and not suitable for the children, downfall being a good word to use! Luckily none of us did downfall so we set up the rods with the bait, a rather straggly worm and attached it to a float and cast in. There must have been around five other fishermen and we noticed that they were getting much more interest than us, we also noticed that they were not float fishing so it was time to re-think our fishing strategy. There was a single man fishing not too far away from us so Lance thought it might be in our favour to ask a local on the best method and of course what fish they catch. He was gone for a good twenty minutes chatting and came back with a whole load of freebees that the gentleman had given us, very generous indeed. We learned that we were going about things all wrong and after setting up the new ledger rig we had been given and baiting up as advised with both a worm and a red sparkly marshmallow we cast out with renewed hope of a meal of trout or if we were very lucky a salmon.

We had never fished using the ledger method and indeed we had never used sparkly marshmallows either so it all seemed a little strange to us. To our amazement within a very short space of time we had actually caught two nice size trout. Why we doubted the method in the first place I do not know but the local's usually know best and they were not wrong. Two fish was enough for a meal so we packed up and went off to find a suitable spot to camp for the night.

The camping spots at Libby Dam are free so saving around twenty-six dollars per night was a big bonus for us. The chosen site was tucked away in the trees next to the river and the rangers at each camp spot had provided a huge pile of firewood so if we wished we could have a good campfire going. We had become used to having a roaring campfire and Libby would be no exception so as well as a free meal, a free camping spot and the use of free firewood, Could that place get any better? Well yes it could as a matter of fact as we were to find out from the ranger who came by to check we were ok and to let us know that a couple of raccoon's lived near by so she advised us to be aware of them and not to leave food or drink around or to leave the door of the motor home open.

The raccoon's had become well socialised to people and they had been known to actually invite themselves in for dinner.

Other than the raccoon's there was not really any other animal that could cause us any problems, it was still early in the shoulder season and the bear's had not yet come down to lower ground so an encounter with a bear was very unlikely.

I can remember the following events quite well as I nearly jumped out of my skin, I was occupied setting up a rod with a spinning lure to have a cast or two in the river and at the same time trying to get rid of the huge red ants that had started to engulf the picnic table I was sat on. I suddenly heard a rather loud noise in the trees beside me and my initial response was to retreat rather quickly from whatever had made such a loud noise, I was having flash backs of elk and bears at that point and was rather concerned about my safety. After a few minutes of gathering myself together I noticed a small face staring down at me from the tree, it was of course one of the racoon's and a second raccoon soon came into view and stood on its back feet in a begging motion less than two meters away. By then the children had been told and we were all watching that cute animal beg for food, we obliged by giving it some crackers despite the rangers warnings not to feed them. Our feeding hour was interrupted by a strange van that had parked up behind the motor home and the raccoon's decided to depart up the tree and temporarily out of sight.

Our visitor was the gentleman who Lance had spoken to at the fishing spot near the dam, he had come to say hello to us all and introduce himself. We learned that night his name and what he did for a living in Libby. We still keep in touch with him by e-mail and of course we hope to go back to Libby sometime in the future to catch up with him and cast a few lines together. After an hour or so of chatting it was time to call it a day and with the raccoons completely gone we turned in for the night.

The next day was just as glorious and we planned to have a go and catch some more fish. We had run out of bait so a trip to the local tackle shop was needed and that short journey would in itself hold a big shock.

The road from Libby Dam to Libby town was well sign posted for deer crossing points so it was always wise to slow down slightly just in case there was a deer waiting to jump into the path of the vehicle you were driving. That may sound rather unlikely, let me assure you it is very likely and after a few miles I noticed out the corner of my eye a deer on the side of the road. That particular deer had taken it upon itself to cross the road at the same point that I was actually on and of course it ran straight into the front of the now emergency braking motor home! A collision was unavoidable and after a big bang and skidding to a standstill Lance quickly got out to check firstly if there was any damage to the motor home and secondly to check on the state of the deer that was lying on the side of the road. The impact was quite hard and we were quite surprised that there was no damage to the front of the motor home and even more surprised when the deer got up, jumped over a five-foot fence and ran off! It was a huge relief that we had not had a more serious collision or that we might have been faced with a dead deer to dispose of, although I suppose we could have had a few venison meals from it!

The rest of the day was spent fishing, playing football with the children and generally taking it easy. We moved location for the second night, as the previous nights spot had been taken by some other happy campers but that was fine, the new spot was just as nice and private. We had the pleasure of our new fishing buddy again that evening and with a roaring fire to keep the mosquitos away we sat for many hours and talked about the world and our different lives. It was a real nice experience to learn about another person's culture and beliefs and of course to share our own with him.

Our time at Libby was over far too quickly and it was time to leave all too soon, much to our regret but we promised ourselves we would definitely return again one day. Montana was a really nice State with many beautiful spots, places you could quite easily spend a month rather than just two days. Our month away was coming to its end and we were slowly winding down our holiday and making our way back up towards the American/ Canadian border.

With Libby still firmly in our heart and our mind we hoped to find another place of pure beauty again before we boarded the flight back home. I cannot truly remember how we found out about Two Medicine Lake that was on the way to Browning but to my knowledge I think someone we spoke to on our travels had recommended that we went there.

The road to the lake was long and we did at one point consider turning back as it was slightly off route and we had a deadline to meet. We were happy that we had not taken that decision, as the place was again one of the most beautiful places we had come across. Surrounded by mountains the lake was a pristine example and a wonderful fishing place, or so we had been told. Two Medicine gets it name from the Blackfeet Indian tribes that lived in those parts and believed the lake held medicinal qualities. The descendents of those tribes still live in the area and Browning further up the road is in the Blackfeet Indian Reserve. The Blackfeet tribes that once lived and hunted there had also named the surrounding mountains, one of which was called Rising Wolf Mountain. The area still held some sort of power that is hard to describe and it was easy to imagine those first settlers setting up camp in such an abundant location.

Grizzly bears were common in the area but at that time of year they were only just coming out of hibernation and still high up in the mountains so the chance of seeing one was rare. It was relaxing to know that we could fish without the worry of a hungry bear finding our catch inviting! Catch was a good word to use as the lake yielded well and we caught three different types of trout, rainbow, lake and brown.

Our newfound buddy in Libby had advised us well with his advise on the use of worms and a sparkly marshmallow as it was a hit with the fish there as well. We lost more than we caught but by evening the abundance of trout in the lake was clear with the amount rising for flies on the surface. It was a fishing paradise, a real gem of a place that you could spend holiday upon holiday at.

Like Libby we spent a second night surrounded by the amazing scenery of that part of Montana and again promised ourselves that we would return. Those two days flew by and we waved goodbye to Two Medicine Lake, it was time to continue to our next stop Kalispell. Our intention was to stay at Kalispell but after seeing the size of the place and the fact that our carbon monoxide detector kept on going off due to the high traffic volume we drove on. Car pollution was obviously high and the only campground we could find there was right next to the main highway so we decided to carry on and find a more suitable camp.

Hungry Horse was the next spot and it was a nice quaint little place, the local campsite was not hard to find and was nestled in pleasant surroundings. It was too late to explore that evening so we stayed in, cooked our freshly caught Two Medicine Lake trout and had an early night all round. All the driving can take it out of you so some early nights were needed.

The next day slightly less refreshed than we had hoped for we set off to have a look at Hungry Horse Dam and maybe find a nice location for a second nights camp. The road going up to the dam was slightly hairy and twisty but we had come across roads worse than that during the trip so we were not too concerned.

After a fairly long drive around the other side of the lake we found a really nice camp spot, the camping areas were not owned as such but wild and payment was made by posting your money in an envelope into a wooden box. Rangers did visit and monitor the camp spaces but it was really an in the wilds place and not too many rangers were seen. The road to the camp spaces was muddy and not a well kept track but it led down to the lake and the whole setting was picture perfect, clear water to swim in and private pitches to pull your camper into. It would have been an ideal place to stop for the night but unfortunately the nicest space next to the lakes edge was taken and the next available space was a little too far away from the lake for comfort. We had noticed a sign on the deposit box stand that the area was well inhabited with grizzly bears and the dense forest just reinforced that. As we had no bear spray or any other means of defending ourselves we decided not to stay there. If we were swimming or relaxing next to the lake and a bear did come by we would have had little chance to make it back to the motor home. It was a sensible idea and the best one despite the disappointment we felt, it was such a lovely spot but just too wild for us without any protection.

We turned around and went back towards Hungry Horse. The children had been asking for a paddle so we stopped at the next lake along called Lion Lake and the children had the opportunity to have their paddle and for Josh and Lance to have a quick swim. I am not too keen on lake swimming or sea swimming for that matter as I have a phobia of what might be lurking in the water. Lion Lake was very murky and it took a great effort on my behalf just to go in shin deep and help Laura and Elijah. After maybe an hour the children had enough soaking and with prune hands and feet we made it back to the campsite we had stayed in the previous night.

We made sure that we got a better spot, one that was not on such a slope as it does aid your sleep if you are not being pushed by gravity into your pillow all night. It was also slightly hard to eat your food as it was sliding off the table before you could get it into your mouth. Not what you want when you have not got a personal washing machine!

After a much better night of sleep and a bowl of steady cereal we had a quick look around the town of Hungry Horse and after purchasing a few souvenirs and some cheap DVD's we made our way out of Hungry Horse and towards Glacier National Park. On arrival we paid the Park fees and looked forward to travelling up the magnificent "Going to the Sun Road". Many had told us that it was a really beautiful pass and aptly named. We visited the small selection of shops at West Glacier and found that the parking was rather on the limited side and the few spaces that were available were only big enough for mini cars. As we are the persevering type we entered one car park that at first glance did not seem too bad and it was a rather bad decision as once we had committed to it we could not reverse and it became clear that our twenty-eight foot motor home was about twenty-two foot too long for the car park! If you can imagine trying to turn a bus around a corner that would be a struggle for a family size saloon then you can picture our dilemma. With Lance driving and I running from window to window at the back shouting slow, go and stop in a rather frenzied fashion we managed to navigate out of the car park and both breathed a huge sigh of relief that we had not smashed our way out leaving a trail of carnage behind us. Our comfort and confidence in driving such a big vehicle took a slight dent after that and we did not want to hang around much longer or to be a further comedy show for the many onlookers that had been watching from a distance.

It was lunch time by then and with slightly embarrassed ego's we made our way up the road past Lake McDonald and stopped in a lay by for a sandwich and a well deserved cup of tea. Although at that point I am sure we both could have done with a shot of something stronger to steady those nerves but a cuppa did the trick.

We were quite disappointed with the whole area as it was a real tourist trap and the lake although scenic was not at its best at all. It was very windy and the lake was a choppy brown coloured froth not at all like the clear blue waters we had seen earlier in the trip. The car park episode and the new finding that our motor home was too big to go up the "Going to the Sun Road" or Logan's Pass as it is better known put a real dampener on the day and added to the disappointment. After our lunch Lance thought it would be a good idea to have a fish in the lake, if we were to achieve nothing else that day maybe a fish or two for dinner would be a bonus. Due to the choppy waves and the wind blowing in our direction fishing was not good. In fact casting out more than a metre was just impossible and when the line did go that bit further the line along with the bait was washed back to the shore within a matter of a few seconds. That particular area of Glacier National Park had not been a kind place for us and after a short drive up to the no go sign for big vehicles we turned around and left for the journey out of Montana and back to the Canadian border for the last leg of our tour.

It actually took us a day less than our planned schedule to arrive back at the Canadian border that I have to say was a lot less stressful than the American equivalent. That is not to say the Canadian border security officers were lax, they were also well equipped to deal with any problems and I am sure well trained to act if necessary.

Arriving at the border and re-entering Canada a day early was a little disappointing as it was an extra day that we could have stayed at Libby or Two Medicine Lake but we were not to know and it was a learning curve for the future. It is always better to arrive slightly early than to arrive too late, that is what I have always been taught as my father is a stickler for good time keeping.

The lower part of Alberta through Cardston towards Calgary was one of those bleak places to us and we travelled swiftly through those areas. I have mentioned in the book in an earlier section about the emigration programmes that we used to watch on the television. Well one of those programmes featured a couple that had set up their new home in Okotoks, just south of Calgary. Okotoks at the time we visited was going through a period of major construction of both residential and commercial building. It was there at the main shopping centre that we came across the best supermarket we had ever been into, a well-known supermarket chain in Canada that unfortunately we cannot directly name. I can go as far to say that they credit themselves as providing the best produce and bakery, they also had wonderful cake sampling when we were there much to the delight of the children and us really. For those who are familiar with Canadian superstores I will give you a clue, the first letter in their name is the nineteenth letter of the alphabet! This will leave you with two choices but I can say no more, sorry. It sounds rather strange that one of the highlights of the holiday was to find such a good supermarket but it truly was and we made the most of the fresh cakes and tarts by buying more than we should have!

We had only two nights of our Canadian holiday left and we had planned to stay in a campsite within a half an hour drive of Calgary. We did not know that the area had received an enormous amount of rain and despite the flood signs we attempted to get to the out of the way campsite. The road was very narrow and not the best road to reverse on turn around on or to have met another vehicle on. Firstly we met another vehicle and the occupants of the car told us that the campsite was under inches of water so no good at all. When they had passed we had to reverse back up the winding road in order to have enough room to achieve the third challenge of turning around on a wider section. With all of those near impossibles complete we headed further in towards the city in search of a camp for our final two nights. The campsite we found was not the best and expensive but we had little choice, it was the only one in the area and easy to find, despite the cost and the fact that the place was heaving it was suitable for the purpose of getting packed and cleaning the motor home ready to return it back to the hire company.

The last two days soon went by and it was time once again to battle our fears and drive back into the big city of Calgary. With

Lance behind the steering wheel we nervously drove on and to our surprise found the motor home company with relative ease. All was well and after receiving our damage waiver deposit back and unloading the cases from the motor home and packing them into the mini bus we headed for the airport. We had spent more or less a whole month in Canada and admittedly we felt it was time for home. Holidays are great but it is always nice to get back home. For us we had only a short while left at home when we got back and still had some final arrangements to make for our New Zealand adventure.

Our last two days and our very last night were not spent at the campsite near Calgary as planned; no we had an extra two days and a night in Canada that was spent at Calgary Airport. Our scheduled flight was cancelled twice due to engine trouble, the last thing you want to hear when you will be in mid air on a plane for eight hours! I have watched many a program were some poor souls get their flight cancelled and I have to admit I have had a good chuckle at their expense. When the boot is on the other foot it is not so funny and living in a busy airport for more than a day is quite unnerving. The airline could not be faulted really and looked after us well by providing free meal vouchers to be used in the airport canteen areas.

Eventually we boarded the flight two days later than expected and made our way back home, tired and in need of a good meal and a good sleep in our own beds. New Zealand was only a few weeks away and we still had work to do.

A Very Long Journey

At this moment in time you may be wondering what indeed we were doing and where we were planning on going, I will forgive your confusion. The truth of the matter is, for us anyway, once you have gone through a month after month hard slog, eight months in our case, finding out you have to wait at least two years does not agree with your plans. After the piles of paperwork, phone calls, e-mails and repeat phone calls and e-mails the thought of staying in a country you have worked so hard to leave for the last eight months does not bring a feeling of joy but rather the opposite. Once that very important pack that has kept you up for hours on end and caused severe headaches, insomnia and not to mention the husband and wife feuds has finally gone you may physically remain in your home country but your mind is following your package and your dream. You become distant and detached from your everyday routine and the easiest of things can turn into a huge ordeal. Patience becomes very unfamiliar and you turn into well a sort of moody delinquent.

We knew that we could not hang around in the UK moping around for the next two to three years, so it was back to the books and the Internet to find a short-term solution. It was at that point that our family and friends thought that we where definitely several sandwiches short of a picnic, the crazy Baird family who have finally succumbed to the stresses and strains of the previous months. "Why, you may ask?" Well a short-term solution to some people in our situation would be to move to Spain, France or Portugal; you know one of those countries within an easy three-hour flight. Oh no not us, instead we opted for a thirty-two hour leisurely hike across to the other side of the world, the furthest place you can possibly go, the home of the kiwi and the famous All Blacks.

New Zealand did not just appear in our heads and we thought ah lets go there; we had briefly looked at New Zealand in the early stages of our emigration plans. What I mean by briefly is we did send off for a brochure and we looked at a few sites on the Internet and thought that it looked like a nice place, to be perfectly honest that is really how far we went.

Each month Lance received a copy of the New Scientist magazine and we always flicked through the job adverts at the back just in case an amazing job opportunity would arise and most months they did not. However in May 2005 it finally happened and there it was staring at us in black and white, an advert from a New Zealand based agency requiring Medical Laboratory Scientists. That was our big chance and we were not going to pass on it.

From that moment on and for the next couple of month's things moved at a rapid rate. Lance simply registered with the agency and was allocated the agent who dealt with Medical Laboratory Scientists.

From memory Lance had to send copies of his degree certificate, transcript and relevant work experience to them so that they could verify that he was genuine. We did not mind that or find it a chore as we had many copies of these documents in our permanent residence in Canada file plus we were used to having to send things off. Once they had verified his information they sent by e-mail a list of positions available within New Zealand that were relevant to Lance's qualifications and experience.

We had not stipulated to the agency any particular locations we would prefer other than we did not want to live in one of New Zealand's big cities. Whether it was the North or the South Island did not matter to us at that time. Of the first list of jobs that came through from the agency only two positions matched Lance's criteria, so we expected to be waiting some time for a job offer. Lance's agent had advised him that the Laboratory Manager of one of the positions had informed her that he was only willing to look at employing New Zealand citizens or residents initially and if he had no success there then he would look at outsiders. We decided only to apply for the last remaining position. Basically what happens is the agency has a copy of your resume, employment history and references so puts you forward for all the jobs you have chosen to apply for, in our case one! That takes away the hard job of filling in application form after application form, which can be quite daunting. All we could do was sit back and let the agency do their job and wait for any news. Within two weeks we received an e-mail from the agency informing Lance that he had been short listed for an interview along with only one other person who happened to be a kiwi! Straight away we knew he was up against it going on the information we had been provided about the other job but never the less we continued to plan his interview. Obviously it was impossible for Lance to fly all the way to New Zealand for a job interview so a telephone one was arranged. Telephone interviews were all new to Lance and I so he did find it very difficult. The telephone connection was not the greatest so he spent half the time shouting down the line and that must have appeared rather rude to the people on the other end.

Within two weeks Lance heard that he had been offered the position and he in turn accepted it. We did not expect success so soon and it came really at quite an awkward time for us, it could be said that we were caught well and truly unprepared, the lesson here is to make sure you are ready to move quickly in the event that you need too!

Some months earlier we had booked a motor home holiday to Canada for the whole month of June, and yes you can guess Lance's new employer wanted him to start in June! It was rather a difficult position to be in but thankfully the agency explained matters and Lance was given a new start date of August 28th 2005. That gave us just enough time to research our new destination, Gisborne (East Coast of the North Island) and it is the first place in the world to see the sun.

Luckily we managed to arrange for a couple of International Removals companies to come within a few days to give us a quote on shipping our belongings to New Zealand. We had already decided not to send over large items of furniture, beds, and kitchen appliances, as it would be cheaper to buy again over in New Zealand. It was easy enough to go through the house stating in each room what we intended to take with us. I must point out here that we were provided with some false information regarding small electrical items; both removal companies told us that we could not use any small electrical items in New Zealand due to the voltage difference. In the UK the voltage is 240 whereas in New Zealand it is 230. Due to that piece of incorrect information we inevitably gave away most of our small electrical items only to find out that once we were in New Zealand all we needed was an adapter plug and they would have all worked fine! Very annoying. We decided which removal company we were going with within a couple of days after receiving their quotes, as one offered a much better service than the other.

With a good idea of what was going and what was not we now had the hard task of trying to sell what was left, believe me it was staggering the amount of stuff we had collected over the years! We had pretty much decided to advertise the larger appliances, furniture and larger electrical items in the local newspaper and the local post office allowed us to place an A4 size poster in the window of those larger items that were for sale. When we came to sell the larger items we advertised them well in advance about four to six weeks and we stated on the adverts that a deposit would secure the item for pick up the day before we were due to leave. That method did work very well as we knew most of the more expensive larger items were sold at a reasonable price. If we had left those items to be sold at the last minute we would have been putting ourselves under pressure as the items would then have needed to be sold quickly to our disadvantage. That is when we would have really lost out financially by letting things go for free or for very little money. We had to learn how to haggle to get the best second hand price but at the end of the day emigration is an expensive business and we needed as much money as we could get.

With deposits taken on the majority of the larger items we planned a garden sale at our house, again we advertised it a couple of weeks in advance of our intended sale date. That gave people time to plan ahead and enquire about the items that we had for sale. We had to ask the local shops and supermarkets to see if we could put an advert up on the notice board, as that is where the majority of people will see that you are having a sale.

Once all the advertising was done we sorted through the items, getting them in order in easily accessible places so we could arrange them quickly the day before the sale. It was now a case of waiting for the big day to arrive and we were optimistic that it would be a success. We had received many phone calls regarding the sale and our adverts had gone into a large number of shops so it all looked good. We must have spent hours the day prior to the sale arranging all the items on tables inside and outside the house, labelling everything with prices and although that is a tedious job it does help if people see how much things are as asking can always be a bit daunting for some and could put them off!

The big day arrived and up we got bright and early. My parents were babysitting the children up at the farm for the day which took the stress away of having them mingling with strangers and we had roped Lance's mum into helping with the hoards of people that we envisaged would turn up. The scene was set, the items all nicely presented on tables with prices. Our sale started at 12pm and finished at 3pm, plenty of time to do well. I would like to be able to tell you that we did a roaring trade, beating people off with sticks, empty tables and a full money tin. Well I am sorry to disappoint but we had only a small handful of prospective purchasers turn up who did not purchase. The only ones who did purchase were family friends who probably bought items because they felt sorry for us and the fact that it was plainly obvious to see that the sale was a complete flop!

For us it was a big effort for little reward and very disheartening. We still had boxes and boxes of stuff to get rid of and a short time in which to do that. Despite our bad luck it cannot be said that all house sales end in disaster and it is always worth giving it ago.

The next plan of attack was to go and try and sell the items at a car boot sale. There was a mega car boot sale each weekend in Rhyl a few miles away so it was an opportunity not really to be missed; it was also a case of having not much choice in the matter. My opinion has always been that people love a bargain and that car booter's usually made a few quid. In reality people love a give away and car booter's, us in this case made not much at all, at least we had enough to buy a bacon sandwich each at the greasy spoon. Again for those unfamiliar with a car boot sale it is exactly that, a sale of items that you brought in your car to sell. Some even leave the items in their car boot so the name car boot sale fits the picture very well.

People really were not willing to spend their pennies that day or the following week as that was not much better. Luckily our family and friends took great pity on us again and took off our hands a large proportion of our unsold items. Items I am sure they really did not need but it was a very kind gesture that we were grateful for.

The car selling also faired poor and with little more than a week left to go before our big move we were getting rather worried that they would not sell. The hassle of selling them through a garage when we were going to be in a different country was just not practical at all. So for the second time we decreased the asking prices on both cars, we really were giving them away. Yet again our family and friends jumped in and bailed us out. My Renault Laguna was eventually bought by Lance's friend in Llangollen and the Ford Mondeo was bought by Lance's best friend's father who subsequently wrote the car off after a couple of months! The local charity shops must have thought it was

Christmas everyday for a period of two weeks as we unloaded boxes upon boxes of unsold items on to them. I am sure that they could have opened another shop solely to sell our stuff.

With the majority of our belongings now gone it was time to concentrate on our farewell party. The party was to be held on the Saturday just under a week before we were due to leave for New Zealand on the following Friday (12th August 2005). There was no way that I was going to endure a long haul flight with a banging headache and the feeling of nausea all of the way.

Luckily for us most of our family and friends lived within a short drive from our home so most of them would be able to attend. I think that the only person who did have to travel was my school friend who at the time lived in London but her parents only lived ten minutes away from us so she had a place to stay.

In my opinion a Saturday is a good day to have a party as people do not have to worry about work the next day, plus like us some like to chill out on a Friday night with a movie and a couple of bottles of the red stuff. We asked those who would be coming to bring a couple of bottles and a plate or two of food, nothing fancy or expensive, just a selection of sandwiches, dips and sausage rolls, food that was easy to prepare, eat and tasted good! We had not saved up tons of money so it was not realistic for us to afford all of the food and drink ourselves. We had to keep that pride at bay and ask for help but our nearest and dearest really did not mind helping out at all.

The big party was a huge success; it was great seeing all the people close to us together in one place. It was a good opportunity for all to catch up with each other's lives and for those to meet the other members of our clan that they had not yet met along with old school friends meeting our parents after some years. I can tell you that some tales were told and many laughs shared. It was such a great atmosphere, everyone enjoying themselves whilst enjoying the food and drink. I have to admit despite the jolly mood there was a tinge of sadness to the event shared I am sure by all. It was the last time that we were going to see some people for a long time. The three children thoroughly enjoyed themselves and that was a delight for all to see. They were in for a big ride over the next few months and although we had explained things to them they were oblivious really to what was happening.

After party day, it was time to reflect on the life in Denbigh that we were about to leave behind. Many a thought for those who could not attend due to other commitments or unforeseen circumstances and of course for those family and friends who were no longer with us. It has to be said that that those last few days were very difficult. My Grandmother was unable to attend the party due to ill health; after all she was in her eighties at that time, so it was important that we saw her before we left. It was nice to spend a good couple of hours with her, chatting about old times gone by, it was also a good time to get some nice pictures of her and the children together. We all knew that it would probably be the last time we would see her and although she put on a brave face and asked, "It will be a long time before I see you again?" I think she also knew she would not see us again. Sadly we were right.

The International Removal Company arrived bright and early on the 11th August 2005 and to our amazement they had only sent one guy to pack up all of our belongings. One guy that was expected to carry out all that work on his own, even more amazing was the fact that he hardly moaned once the whole time. He really deserved a medal as by mid afternoon he had boxed everything and packed it all onto the lorry.

Our last full day in our three-bedroom semi detached in Denbigh, North Wales, UK was spent double-checking our documents. Checking we had our flight tickets and passports all together and labelling our suitcases, the last minute sort of stuff you have to do to make sure all is in order. It was probably the fifth time we had checked everything but I suppose it helped with the stress. We had a few visitors that day; Lance's parents came to say their last goodbyes and to take some photographs of us all in front of our house. Both cars were picked up along with all the items that a deposit had been taken for a few weeks previous. The house looked very bare without all our furniture and belongings in it and it had a strange echo about it that all empty properties have. We hoped that it would not be too long until we could have all our possessions back in a new home in New Zealand. Unfortunately our biggest financial problem that was our house had not yet sold, despite several viewings no one had committed to a firm offer and it was unlikely that an offer would come on the last day. We had foreseen that problem occurring a couple of weeks prior to us leaving so I sought some advice from my solicitor to see if we could put the house sale into the hands of my parents. To sell the property from New Zealand would have been virtually impossible as there was quite a large amount of paperwork to be signed so it would have not been realistic. It really was a simple case of my solicitor drawing up a document that stated that we had given power of attorney to my parents and that enabled them to sign the necessary documents on our behalf when the need arose. It was a relief to know that the house sale was in safe hands although it was a huge worry for us. We had hoped to sell the house and have it all done and dusted with the money in the bank before we left but that was just wishful thinking on our behalf.

Our last visitors of the day were my parents who had kindly brought a couple of bottles of white wine to see us through our last evening, hypocrite springs to mind considering I said that I did not want to have a drink the night before our flight! I let myself off with the notion that our flight was not until 8pm the next evening so any small hangover would be well and truly gone. After a few glasses and a reminisce Dad and Linda went home and left us to have our last nights sleep on a fold out bed chair. Laura and Josh's bed's were going up to be stored at dad's along with Elijah's cot so at least they had a good nights sleep in their own bed. Not a comfort we had so as you could imagine a good night sleep was not on the agenda.

On the 12th August 2005, we left our family and friends at the airport terminal and headed through customs towards the departure lounge. With bleary eyes and plenty of soggy tissues we boarded our flight and left the United Kingdom for our destination of Auckland, New Zealand.

Kiwi Land

Our flight touched down at the Auckland International Airport shortly before 2.40pm on Sunday 14th August 2005, taking the one stop and time difference into account we arrived two days after we left the UK.

We left the airplane with matchstick eyes and in a state of complete exhaustion. The three children had been wonderful throughout the whole journey, the penalty of keeping them amused was indeed lack of sleep but they could have created the whole time, they were great. We did try to take turns to sleep but it was very hard when you know your other half is also very tired and what brief sleep we did manage to gain was of little quality. However despite our feelings at that time we had arrived and we had to concentrate on getting quickly through New Zealand customs and having a good meal and a very good nights sleep at the hotel.

New Zealand Custom's was relatively easy, all our documents were in order and we had a copy of Lance's accepted job offer so we were given a six-month visitor's visa. I have to fill you in a bit here, as at that point we did not have a work permit/visa to enter New Zealand as we had hoped. Due to our Canadian holiday and the short space of time afterwards we did not have enough time to finalise Lance's work permit/visa before leaving. The agency in New Zealand informed us that it would be acceptable to finalise the paperwork when we arrived. Unfortunately the agency had once again given us the wrong information and it turned out that it would take a while longer to sort things out so more on that shortly!

Our hotel offered a courtesy shuttle service for guests and they promptly collected us from the airport within ten minutes of us phoning to say we had arrived. It was such a relief to have a sit down and a nice hot cup of tea, chill out and relax in our own company and space! I think not having freedom of space on such a long flight is very hard to cope with especially when you are used to being relatively free do what you please in your own home. It was around 3.30pm by then and our plan of attack for the evening was to have a short sleep and then go to have some food in the restaurant. Our plan of attack was about to go not quite as we planned or rather not at all as we planned. We woke up quite a few hours later, the children were all still fast asleep and we felt totally shattered, the new plan of attack was to forget about our grumbling tummies and go straight back to sleep. The next time any of us stirred was 9am the next morning; we had literally slept none stop for hours and we had worked up quite an appetite! After our sleep marathon we hastily got dressed, showered and headed for the breakfast room. The staff could not believe how much cereal, toast, croissants and anything else edible we consumed. We did feel rather piggy so explained that we had had little food for quite a few hours and we were very hungry! After our breakfast feast we felt much brighter and ready for the internal flight to Gisborne.

The previous day we had stepped of a huge Boeing 747, so we were rather shocked when we were directed out onto the tarmac towards our Gisborne flight, a very small little aircraft in comparison. The flight itself only took an hour but it was a rough ride, the craft was so small you could hear every bang and squeak; the turbulence was rather awful although the craft flew low enough for us to see the land below so close, it was nerve wracking.

Eventually we descended into Gisborne airport and we were surprised how small the airport was but nevertheless we had finally arrived at our new home. It took less than five minutes to de board our toy plane and meet Lance's new boss who was there to meet us along with a work friend who had lived in Gisborne for thirty years and was previously from Yorkshire, UK. I have to say here and Lance will agree, we could not quite believe the fact that they had lived in New Zealand all those years and still sounded like they had just arrived from the Yorkshire Dales, amazing!

It was a short journey to our accommodation at the hospital that had been provided as part of the relocation package. A three-bedroom flat they called it but it was more like a detached bungalow that looked lovely from the outside with a massive grassed area for the children to play, we would enjoy it there! The huge feeling of relief of arriving and the luck of being allocated such nice accommodation left us as quickly as a bolting horse when the stable door is left open. We walked into a filthy dirty house, it needed a good clean before we could settle properly and that was the last thing we felt like doing. The next few days were spent washing the flat from top to bottom, cupboards, drawers and windows that had grown a nice amount of mould, it really was disgusting. Our first impressions of New Zealand were to say the least not the best, feeling so tired due to Jet Lag and having to undertake such intense cleaning duties did contribute a lot to our negative feelings.

Once the flat was cleaned to our standards and all the suitcases were unpacked it was time to start concentrating on the
visa/permit situation that was somewhat of a not too funny joke
in itself. Firstly we were told by the agency that Lance should
apply for a work to residence permit and that all the rest of the
family would be covered on his visa, wrong, we had to apply
individually for our own permits. I had to apply for a work permit, Josh had to apply for a student permit and Laura and Elijah had to apply for a visitor's permit. That was totally
unexpected and very costly. Luckily the Immigration section in
Wellington acted quickly and we received our permits within a
week, although our passports and application forms were sent
via courier so that speeded it up. I would like to point out here
again that the information I have provided in this section is
based on our experiences only and should not be taken as legal
advice. The processes can change at any time. For those readers
unfamiliar with the New Zealand visas and permits and what
they both mean I will briefly cover them now.

> Work, Visitor's and Student Permits—These allow you to
> visit, work and study in New Zealand legally for the period
> stated on your permit and work in the occupation you have
> stated on your application. They are an obvious require-
> ment, without one you will be in the country illegally and
> you would be removed.

> Work, Visitor's and Student Visas—These visas allow you
> to leave New Zealand say for a holiday and re-enter after
> that time away. If you intend to re-enter New Zealand you
> must have a Multi Entry visa. This is very important, as
> without that visa you will not be able to re-enter New
> Zealand!

Medicals/X-rays and police clearances are also required. A doctor that can be found on the New Zealand Immigration website must carry out the medicals, as our own doctor could not do them.

The basic rule is you need a permit to be in the country, you need a visa to be able to leave the country and re-enter. You do not have to get the visa at the same time as your permit, however dependent on which permit you apply for you may get them together anyway. Lance and Josh got their permit and visa automatically at the same time. Laura, Elijah and I did not so we had to apply for one when we were going to leave for a holiday outside of New Zealand. Obviously you have to pay an extra fee for the visa's hence why we did not apply for one straight a way. It sounds confusing but once we understood what was required it was pretty easy.

Lance had been told that it would be easier to apply for a Work to Residence permit and that is were the confusion for us set in! Basically that is a normal work permit, however the difference is after two years you can gain permanent residence. We were informed by the agency that permanent residence was automatically granted after that two-year period was up, that easy! Well in fact it was another load of rubbish we had been told again by the agency! We eventually found out from the New Zealand Immigration that permanent residence was not granted automatically at all but you had to apply for it and that meant starting from scratch and a whole new set of medicals and police checks had to be carried out again. How infuriating, we had spent a lot of money having medicals in the first place and we did not expect to have to undertake them again. If we wanted to apply for a Work to Residence permit we were all required to have a second medical at our cost if we applied for permanent residence two years after we gained our Work to Residence permit. That is admittedly confusing and I still find it hard to believe. The Work to Residence permit seems like a complete waste of time and money to me, it only meant that we would have had to undertake two medicals and two police checks at our expense in a short period of time.

Understandably we were not too happy with the agency and they apologised for causing extra stress due to their wrong information. It has to be said that there is a lot of things to organise even when you have arrived in your new country. All the hard work is certainly not over once you have boarded your flight but what needs doing must be done; there is no other way around it.

After the initial horror of the rancid flat and feeling so down beat about the permit/visa situation things started to look up and we felt more positive about the whole New Zealand thing. Lance's employer had allowed us to borrow the little laboratory car after hours so we could at least explore our new city of Gisborne. I have to say that first impressions were good and the overall feeling of the place was that Gisborne was a friendly place to be with the added bonus of white sandy beaches and the clear blue Pacific Ocean. Gisborne is not a huge city; at the time of our arrival the population was around thirty three thousand. The Gisborne region has a Maori population of over fifty percent so we were prepared to start to learn the language and read up about the history and traditions that in some areas are still practiced. It was all very exiting.

After the first few days of organising ourselves we set about the usual things when you move, organising the phone/internet access and opening a bank account. Those were arranged with relative ease and we were feeling that we had started to get established. Lance was shown around the laboratory and met his new work colleagues that were welcoming to him so that was a good start. Not all the staff in the laboratory were New Zealanders, quite a few were from South Africa so there were lots of cultural differences that would make his job interesting to say the least. It was good timing on our behalf as one of the guys was selling a Subaru station wagon and we were in need of a cheap run around, the car was ok and we went ahead and bought it. Our very own set of wheels we called Sue the Subaru!

With Lance now in work it was time to start looking for a school for Josh and a Kindergarten for Laura. In New Zealand children start school at five years old unlike the UK were the school starting age is four. That meant that Laura was taking a step backwards with regards to schooling as she had attended a school in Denbigh prior to our departure.

The flat was ours for the first month and due to rental properties in short supply in Gisborne at that time our period of time in the flat was extended. As I explained earlier we had not sold our house in Denbigh before we left the UK but luckily after our first week in New Zealand a reasonable offer was made and we accepted. It was a huge weight of our shoulders and the house sale meant we could start to look at buying a property instead of renting. We were fortunate that we did not look too hard and find a property we really liked as within a few days we received a call from Dad with the devastating news that the buyer had pulled out of the deal. We were back to square one again with little option to persevere and find a rental property for the time being.

Finding a school for Josh was easy enough as some of Lance's work colleagues had children of a similar age and they recommended a school near by. We made an appointment and had a chat with the head teacher and we were taken for a tour of the school grounds. It was a nice school with good qualities so Josh was enrolled the same day to start on the following Monday.

Things were finally settling down into a routine and that really helps the settling in process. We still had the UK house sale hanging over our heads but what could we do, it was a matter of waiting until a genuine buyer came along, the waiting was agony. By now are first month in New Zealand was over and it was time to start paying the rent on the flat. It was fortunate for us that the rent included the electricity and water charges so it was just about manageable for us. We knew that time was running out with the flat and we had to find a rental of our own so we contacted a rental company in Gisborne and it was not long before we were viewing potential properties. The big problem for us was a lot of the properties the company had were expensive and we were not in a position were we could afford a large monthly rent and pay for our UK mortgage also. Eventually the company came up with the goods and found us a lovely three-bedroom home in a very sort after area of Gisborne. The sort of area where your neighbours are vets and doctors! In fact the owners of the rental we had chosen were airline pilots so it was an executive area.

We were grateful for the extension of time that we had at the hospital flat, it served its purpose in providing adequate accommodation once cleaned. Without that extension we would have been renting a place in cardboard city. It was time to stand on our own two feet and take on the real challenge of our own rental property and more to the point the challenge of affording it! To be honest for the location of the house the rent was very good and well below some of the other places we looked at in the less desirable areas. The big bonus for us and a big factor in taking the property was it had fishing access at the bottom of the garden and for keen fisher people like ourselves what more temptation could we want. So it was time to pack up our measly belongings and move to Marian Drive.

Getting Settled in New Zealand

Our new rental provided us with the first proper place we could call home. It was not really ours but it felt better than living in temporary accommodation and for the first time since we had arrived in New Zealand we finally felt things were going well for us. Josh was settled in school and enjoying it and I had found Laura a kindergarten within easy walking distance from our house and she attended each morning for a few hours.

Our belongings finally arrived after three months at sea so we once again had familiar items around us. The rental house was furnished so we did not have to go out and buy all the big items of furniture or large appliances and that was a huge relief let alone a big cost that we did not have to worry about. The only thing that was missing was a bank full of money, the money from our UK house sale that had not happened yet. Maybe that was about to change for the better as within the first week of being in the rental we accepted another offer on our property, surely that time we would have a successful sale. The process went smoothly and things were looking promising, we really thought that the sale was going to happen. For the second time and to our despair the house sale fell through, the buyer could not get finance. It was all turning into a big bad joke that was causing us a great deal of stress. It became apparent that the rent combined with our UK mortgage payment was just unafford-able to us. There was just not enough money coming in each month to pay for both the rent and mortgage or to simply sur-vive. We had to sell that house or be faced with the true reality of returning with tails between legs back to the UK and back to a life we wanted to escape from.

Two weeks later we accepted a third offer on the house and again it fell through, there was no third time lucky for us. There was also no chance we could stay in that lovely rental any longer; it was just too big a financial strain. After only two short months we left Marian Drive and returned to hospital accom-modation. Lance had told the property manager our plight and he being an understanding fellow provided us with a two bed-room flat. It was a little small for us but newly refurbished, clean and tidy. We would be spending our first New Zealand Christ-mas in hospital accommodation but that was fine, we could have been spending Christmas 2005 back in the UK!

Our first Christmas was very different and we could not get into the Christmas swing of things at all. Lance's work pal's had taken pity on us and bought us a real Christmas tree with a whole big box of decorations, a very kind gesture. The problem for us was it was mid summer. Summer at Christmas time was just not right at all. In our eyes we should have been cold and snug drinking Mulled Wine. Instead we were sat around the dinner table drinking gallons of water stripped down to our underwear with the electric fan on full speed trying to cool us down whilst we were trying to enjoy our festive lunch! It was not a pleasurable experience eating a huge dinner as you do on Christmas Day while feeling as hot as the roasted turkey in front of you that we could all sympathise with. The seasons in New

Zealand are completely the other way around to the UK, it just felt seriously wrong. We had been told that eventually we would get used to it but that was hard to take on board and getting used to it was not yet on our list. Things would definitely take a while longer than we first thought.

On a happier note we had a very nice Christmas present, for the fourth time we accepted an offer on our UK property and although it was well below what we wanted the couple were very keen. We crossed everything that could be crossed in hope that fourth time lucky would prevail and the sale would finally be all done. It did look like it really was good that time. My parents were due to fly to New Zealand at the end of January so it was a big push for all concerned to complete the sale before they left for their months holiday. It was a very big task but we finally got the best news, the news that we had awaited for such a long time. Our UK house had finally sold and the money was in our UK bank. All we had to do then was to transfer the funds to our New Zealand bank account. We used a Money Broker Service; they are all well advertised in the emigration magazines and on the Internet so we had no trouble finding one. Our money was transferred with little trouble within two days of authorising the company to transfer the funds. Banks can take up to a month and they also take a hefty fee out of your money for the privilege.

My parents Arthur and Linda arrived in Gisborne in their hired motor home at the beginning of February and they had planned to spend two weeks with us. It was so nice to see them as we had been away for six months; it was BBQ and party time again! Dad likes a good few glasses of red wine and he won't mind me saying, so when I was in the chemist and noticed a huge wine glass I could hardly resist. It went down a treat and we have a wonderful picture of him holding his huge wine glass that would hold more than a full bottle although even for him that was too much of a mouthful at once.

Their first few days in Gisborne were spent recuperating from the marathon flight that they had endured and by about 7pm they were both looking like they needed eye props and went off to bed. Those who have not been on such a long journey cannot possibly know how hard it is, it really is tough.

The weather in Gisborne had been lovely and hot, summer was coming to an end but it was still nice to go out with short sleeves and shorts. Unfortunately the day that Dad and Linda arrived in Gisborne the weather changed and it rained the whole time they were there. Even more annoying was the day they left us the sun came out again and stayed! We had a good time and a few days out showing them the local attractions and they had a couple of days to themselves sightseeing before they left Gisborne to continue their North Island tour.

With the visit over it was time to get back to house hunting. It had quickly come to light some months previous that our dream of owning our own acreage with animals was not to be. House prices had escalated in Gisborne the past year and we had well and truly missed the boat. We were also realising that affording a reasonable house in the nicer parts of the city were also slowly slipping out of reach. However we still persevered despite feeling rather inadequate on the mortgage front. We could afford a nice vehicle at least and that made us feel slightly better.

We had decided even before leaving the UK what type of vehicle we would buy when we received our money in New Zealand. We had always wanted a 4x4 truck and that is exactly what we were going to have. After all the stress and strain we had endured we deserved it. It did not take us too long to find the perfect vehicle, not cheap but just what we wanted, a Gold Nissan Terrano. Our dream vehicle had been purchased so it was back to the hard job of finding the dream home we would be parking it outside along with Sue the Subaru of course.

We looked at quite a few properties within our budget and funnily enough a lot of the houses were number thirteen, it really was an omen, whether a good one or a bad one remained to be seen. We would buy the newspaper every Thursday and scan through the property pages to hopefully find a nice house in our price range. One particular week a new listing caught our eye and to our amazement it was another number thirteen. The house seemed to jump out at us but due to the description and location it seemed that it would be well out of our price range. Nevertheless I contacted the real estate lady who told me that the property was indeed well within our budget, we could hardly believe it. We learnt that the property was to be sold by Tender, a popular method of selling in New Zealand but very new to us. Basically a date is set by the vendor and on that day they will look at all offers made on the property and decide which offer they will accept. That does not always mean the vendor will accept the highest offer, they may accept a lower offer that has less conditions such as subject to finance or subject to builders inspection.

So two weeks before the set date we put our unconditional offer on the Tender form and posted it into the box. The next two weeks seemed to drag and we had convinced ourselves that we had little hope of winning the Tender. We did see the house three times in those two weeks and absolutely one hundred percent loved it, it was everything we wanted. The big day of reckoning came and when the phone rang I knew it was the realtor to tell us the bad news that the house had sold to someone else for thousands more than our offer. It had not; we had been successful and won the Tender. I could hardly believe it, we had won solely due to the fact our offer was unconditional and not on the amount we had offered, as that had been well beat. I immediately phoned Lance at work and informed him of the good news; he was delighted just like me. No one could take it away from us as in New Zealand once an offer is accepted on a property it is a legally binding contract, to pull out of a deal holds a huge penalty. We finally had our dream car and our dream house; number thirteen was a good omen for us. The move in date was set for six weeks later. It was a longer than usual timescale but the lady selling the house had a few issues and we gave her the benefit of the doubt. The house was ours so if we had to wait a little to move in then so be it. It gave us a chance to hit the shops and start buying some nice furniture.

We were on a huge high, everything since our UK house sale had gone through successfully everything seemed to work out for the best for us. It was a great time for us after our weeks of bad luck.

On Thursday 13th April 2006 that high came down to earth with a huge ton of bricks with news that I had certainly not expected. Lance answered the phone and I knew it was Dad, something was not right as he was due to go away that very morning. I also knew why he had phoned; call it a sixth sense I don't know but I knew. My Grandmother had passed away at home; she had suffered a huge heart attack and died instantly. The news was awful and it was even harder to deal with due to the harsh reality that there was little chance of being able to fly home for the funeral and say a proper goodbye to her. It was the first time we realised just how far away from home we were and it was an uncomfortable feeling. All we could do was send some flowers arranged over the Internet and the three children made a goodbye Nan poster that we sent to Dad. He placed it in her coffin near her face alongside a picture of us all sat together on our sofa in New Zealand when they visited.

Nan's death had given us all a big shock but we still had a new house to move into and we had to move on. Those first few weeks were hard to say the least but we managed to get through one day at a time.

Whether it was somehow due to Nan's death and the slight isolation we were feeling at that time we started to pick up on a lot of negative issues in New Zealand especially Gisborne that really challenged our commitment. The only thing that kept us motivated was the lovely new house we had just bought in a very sought-after secluded part of the city. We had realised that the native New Zealand culture was not what we had first thought and that crime; drug use and gang warfare was higher than we thought in Gisborne and in many other places in New Zealand. You really do have to be very careful what you say these days hence why I am not directly naming here. Having a good honest opinion can land you in a whole heap of trouble. I am sure that we have become far too comfortable with walking on eggshells, too scared to stand up for ones opinions. It is of course human nature to agree and disagree, unfortunately we feel more inclined to agree just in case disagreeing will offend. The slightest well-meaning criticism to an individual, group or race becomes a racist remark. I sometimes wonder if people could speak out and be truthfully honest would there be so much social and political confusion going on in the world? All I can see is the more our voices are smothered the more we fight to be heard, the anger that fuels the fire. Our right to speak freely taken away. I am not saying that that loss of voice is the sole reason to why the world in general is in such a mess but I would sure offer it up as a definite role player.

I think overall we had just started to feel a little homesick and sometimes it is easy to pick up on the negative sides of things when you are in that frame of mind. Hopefully things would settle once again once we had moved into our own place.

The six weeks passed quickly and the May possession date finally arrived. Waiteata Street was for us a dream home after the disappointment of not being able to afford our own acreage. We thought we would have to settle for a mediocre property in a less than ideal place. It was not a huge house but with a very large garden to keep us busy and with the house lay out and storage space well organised it was big enough for us. It took us less than a week to unpack all our boxes and rearrange the furniture until we reached the desired look. It was so nice to sit down on our own sofa in our very own house listening to all the birds in the trees and taking in the peace and quiet of such a tranquil location. It was a good feeling after all the previous months of turmoil. The location of the house could not have been better for Josh and of course for Laura who was by then in her last few weeks of Kindergarten. The school was literally a five-minute walk from the front door.

The first few weeks in our new home were spent ordering some new carpets to replace the threadbare pieces of material in the lounge and hall that I suppose once upon a time deserved to be called a carpet. The décor in the house was fine and we really did not need to do anything to change it. The garden however was a different kettle of fish and required quite a bit of work to bring it up to the Bairds standards! After several trips to the local skip and hours of weeding and digging we finally achieved a reasonably nice garden and vegetable plot. The front garden was pretty much arranged to look after itself, full of perennials and roses. After all the hard work we had reached a point were the house and gardens were very much to our taste.

Although we were happy with the new house and the new garden we could not quite shake off the negative demons. It was not too long before they had established a strong grip on our shoulders and we were once again feeling very torn.

Second Thoughts

We had been in New Zealand for about nine months by that time and to be honest the majority of those nine months were spent wondering what on earth we had done. It really felt at times like a bad mistake. We had put the Canada move into the back of our heads for the time being as we did not know how long we would have to wait to hear anything so we just concentrated on New Zealand life. For once something positive had happened so we had to try and forget all the negative issues and work on the positive ones.

It was around that time that we became friendly with another English family with a son the same age as Joshua. They had also left behind their family and friends in the UK and took the big plunge to live in New Zealand. Gisborne was where the employment was so that is where they headed although they were not new comers to Gisborne as they had lived there for around twelve months prior to us meeting them. They had been more fortunate than us in the luck department as they had managed to purchase a very nice acreage a few minutes drive from the city. We quickly learned that we were not alone in picking up the negative vibes of the place and it was a topic of many conversations we had. They personally felt the South Island would be a much better option for them and I know at the time of writing they were planning that move.

In order to help moral we thought that it would be a good time to invest in a dog. I had a lovely Boxer in the UK some years ago and it was agreed that when we settled into our own place we would get another one. During the months we had been in New Zealand we had gained three extra feline family members called Boo, Tammy and Timmy, Timmy was Boo's kitten. So an extra pet was really not a problem. In fact we thought that having a dog to occupy our spare time might help us with the positive approach therapy. We went ahead as planned and after searching many breeders we finally found Jake, an eight-week-old brindle Boxer dog who was also registered with the New Zealand Kennel Club. He was not from a local breeder so we had to arrange a short flight for him from Auckland to his new home in Gisborne. He was the last thing to be unloaded from the airplane and at one point we did think we had been swindled out of our money but sure enough we soon saw a scrunched up cute little face peering out of the small dog crate and my heart melted, he was gorgeous. As with all new puppies the first few nights were rather fraught for all concerned and admittedly we shouted and balled at Jake to shut up once the interrupted sleep got too much to bare. The howling and whining only lasted a few days and he soon settled down into a routine and became a not so well behaved member of the family! Digging big holes in the back garden did not go down so well after all the hard work we had put into it. The three cats would not accept any messing around as far as they were concerned and Jake got quite a few claws in the face for his pestering so he soon learned that the cats would not tolerate too much harassment and he learned after a while to let them be.

It could be said that we had it good, a nice house and a nice big truck, you know the sort of family that people think are perfect. I do not think any family is perfect but there are those who do appear to be living a very good life. It could have been assumed going on outwardly appearance that we were one of those families. We did not see that at all and even after the run of good luck we still felt very unsettled and we did feel that way for some very good reasons. More and more negatives were appearing in our lives that really were affecting the happiness that we should have been feeling. We were in a huge dilemma about our future. Things could just not continue on that path.

The children were settled into a good routine, Laura and Josh now attended the same school and Elijah had finally settled into his afternoon Kindergarten sessions after much crying and moaning. School for the children was not overly different from that in the UK to be honest, school is school! The main difference was the culture, the children had Maori studies and that was a change from the usual. Swimming in the school pool was a big part of the summer physical education program so again something different for them. They both made friends easily but I suppose young age helps there so all in all the schooling was the same old story. Christmas was only a few months away and we were looking forward to Lance's sister and family who were coming over for the festive period.

To get away for a few days from the relentless negatives that we could not seem to get past we booked into a holiday park in Hastings for a couple of days. A couple of days away would maybe clear the air and give us a few days concentrating on family activities. It was not to be as planned as on the morning we were due to leave I had a call from Linda, my stepmother back on North Wales. Linda rarely phoned so I knew there was something wrong immediately. They had been on a holiday in France for a couple of days, a trip they did regularly on his motorbike. I had sent him a text the night before we were due to set off on our break, as I knew that they had hoped to be back home by that time. It was a text that he never replied to and I found that strange and out of character for him. On the way back from France and on the M6 motorway they had been hit from behind in slowing traffic by quite frankly an idiot on his mobile phone. Dad was thrown twenty feet into the fast lane and suffered horrendous injuries to his arm and wrist along with a broken hip and major bruising. Linda was very lucky escaping with severe bruising and a broken finger although I am sure seeing your husband in a crumpled mess on the road must have been worse than anything.

That phone call for me was the last straw, the final push that I needed to say I cannot stay here and Lance agreed. The majority of the New Zealand experience was just not for us, too many things had gone wrong and I have always believed there are reasons to why things happen. It was not just Nan's death or Dad's accident but since moving into the house we had struggled financially. Dipping into our dwindling savings each month to make ends meet and I am not talking about small amounts either. The financial burden was getting us down; it was really unbelievable to think that Lance was actually on a very high wage and we still struggled each month. I am amazed that those people who were on a lower income could afford to feed themselves let alone rent or own a property. I think the financial side of things were tough also because Gisborne was in itself a very expensive place to live. If you look at Gisborne on a map you will see that it is quite isolated. To get anywhere with decent shops was at least a three to four hour car journey, those of you who have travelled on New Zealand roads will know that some of them are very twisty. It was just an unpleasant journey to

make when it was guaranteed the children would turn green
and be sick, at times even Lance and I had to pull over and get
out for a breath of fresh air! That isolation meant that Gisborne
was expensive compared to other locations in New Zealand and
it was a noticeable difference when we did make the trek to say
Whakatane or Napier. The fortnightly shop was usually above
the two hundred and fifty dollar mark and we were only buying
the necessary items we needed, treats cost extra so were few and
far between. By the time we had shopped, paid the mortgage
each fortnight and forked out for the extra costs in life we had
little money left. We were in a situation were all of our savings
would eventually have been wiped out and we would have had
nothing left. If it were not for the savings account some weeks
we would have been really up the creek without a paddle. The
bailiff's would have been knocking on the Bairds door! Things
were that bad.

As we were only in New Zealand on work permits we were
not entitled to any benefits, however the government still
expected us to pay tax, which I found rather wrong. In my eyes
if we were good enough for tax purposes we were good enough
to receive some extra help in a new country.

On a separate note Lance's job had taken a turn for the worse
over the months. Changes in the laboratory had meant that certain people had been moved into positions that they were inca-
pable of filling. The original laboratory manager had moved
over to a different department and his underdog had been put
into the position of temporary acting manager. Positions of
authority that they were not suitably qualified to do, at all! In
fact that particular person who cannot be named turned into a
manager from hell with very little managerial or social skills.
That caused a huge increase in stress and tension in the work-

place that obviously affected the once happy atmosphere and good level of staff moral. It did not help at all that staff felt they could not complain about the issues important to them or complain about bad treatment as the old laboratory manager and the new acting laboratory manager were pretty much best of friends! They stuck together like glue so any complaints were twisted around and the staff member making those complaints in good faith were in turn being victimized.

The whole laboratory turned into a horrible place to work as people who were once good friends had been turned against each other and tale telling had become high on the list of priorities for some who wanted to earn brownie points with the management. It had got so bad that if you were caught talking you were immediately reprimanded like a school pupil or if a staff member had nothing to do at that particular moment they would be dragged over the coals in the office! It turned into an adult kindergarten and Lance was getting more and more fed up of the juvenile behaviour in the laboratory.

Lance had to work some ridiculous shifts. I still cannot understand how the shifts are not illegal as they honestly were a health risk. The staff were required to work a week of late shifts, 4pm until midnight but then on the Friday they were expected to be on call from midnight until 8am the next morning. It was not unusual for Lance to get home after a late shift on a Friday, get into bed and be called straight back out again. On a few occasions people started work 4pm on the Friday afternoon and did not rest until their shift finished at 8am Saturday morning. That was a huge test both mentally and physically and totally unfair. It was not surprising given all the circumstances Lance was less than happy with his employment, in fact he could not stand it.

Since our move into Waiteata Street the cities varied community problems had increased. Drug use especially methamphetamine drugs such as "P" had become more increased and in turn crime to support that habit had also increased. A very worrying and serious issue when you have children. A house in our street was actually burgled by three fourteen year olds, things were getting a bit too close for comfort especially when we saw the three boys hanging around on numerous occasions. That safe feeling had started to dwindle and I was feeling increased anxiety when Lance was at work during the evenings. Within a space of two months there had been four homicides in Gisborne, an unusual high level in such a small city and a very worrying trend. Gang warfare between the two well-known New Zealand gangs, the Mongrel Mob and Black Power had escalated in recent times in Gisborne with street fighting and stabbings occurring. In truth it was just not the same place we had moved to many months earlier. Either that or we had been suffering from tunnel vision the whole time but I do not believe that for a minute.

One of the biggest issues we had with living in New Zealand was the distance we were away from home, the UK. After Nan's death and Dad's motorbike accident we realised just how far that was as it was just not feasible in time or money to just hop on a plane at the drop of a hat and fly back. If Dad and Linda had been in a worse condition it would of taken me at least two days to get back to the UK and two days can be far too late in serious situations. That was a very true wake up call for us.

In one way we were not alone with all of that negativity. The friends that I mentioned earlier in the book also felt very unsettled at that time. We had discussed moving on numerous occasions both within New Zealand and out of New Zealand, the difference between us was they wanted to settle on the South Island and although we had thought of moving there we would still be a million miles from home and even more isolated than we were in Gisborne. The South Island was very appealing with its mountain ranges and famous landmarks but it was a move we were not prepared to make. Living in a more remote location was not the answer for our family and I am happy that we did not go that way. It would have been a costly mistake for our ever-decreasing bank balance and for us.

Call it fate I do not know but around that same time we received a letter from the Canadian High Commission asking us to submit updated information as they would be processing our application ninety days after the date on the letter. It was totally out of the blue for us and changed our whole outlook on things. We had finally heard from the Canadian High Commission and it was almost as if they had heard our cries for help.

With our Canadian dream finally in sight we set about gathering the documentation that they required. We had not been called for medicals at that time, as they only required details of what we had been doing in the time since we submitted our application back in November 2004. That was when we realised we had not for some reason kept a copy of some of the original forms, a very clever thing to do when they are asking you to re write it all again on new forms! A slight air of panic and the feeling of how stupid we were had taken over. However in times of importance you somehow manage to pull through although I knew without a doubt some of the information would have been slightly different from the original forms. It was a risk we would have to take and hope they would not throw our whole application in the bin for variation of information.

It took us about two weeks to organise the documents together and send them off to the London office. Although we lived in New Zealand at that time we were not residents so our processing office was still in the UK. The distance would mean a slight delay with the postal service but we had waited that long so a few more weeks would not make too much difference!

It was now November 2006 and with Christmas looming it was doubtful that we would hear back from the Canadian High Commission before our visitors and the festivities started. The fact that the London office only works half days did not give us much confidence either so with the new documents sent all we could do was plan a fun filled family Christmas.

We set about planning that fun filled Christmas over the weeks that followed until everything was set, new decorations and Christmas tree bought and a new tent bought to accommodate the extra guests that may want to stay after a few festive drinks. We were ready for Christmas; all that was left was for Lance's sister and family to arrive. The biggest question was that to be our last New Zealand Christmas. The answer was yes.

Decision to Leave

Our decision to leave New Zealand was determined by many factors. All of the negative happenings that had occurred during the time we had spent there and it was important that the decision had not been influenced just on the more recent events of Nan's death or Dad and Linda's accident. Those were huge factors in the decision and I will not deny that but we had to base our leaving on everything that had happened as a whole and look at all the good and the bad points to living in New Zealand.

We had purchased a great house but it became a house that we could not afford on the wages that Lance brought home each fortnight, wages that were a very good salary. We had not gone to New Zealand with the idea that we would be spending our savings just to get by each month and those savings would inevitably run out at some point. We were not impressed with the native New Zealand culture and felt that it had indeed very much lost its way. A disappointing find and a shame to think that the future would surely bring to an end those few that still practised and believed in their way. It was a part of New Zealand and all you read about before arriving but I feel that the only real culture that was to be seen was by actors in the tourist traps around the country. I am not saying all is lost but it is a true and honest opinion that the confidence and will for such an amazing culture has to come back soon in order to save it. New Zealand is a wonderful place full of natural beauty and surrounded by the most amazing oceans but the big price to be paid for that tranquil environment was a huge distance between there and home. That was always in the back of our minds and with that negativity lodged firmly the chance of settling was very low from the start. We had tried hard to give it a good go but with lessening funds, home very far away and the new lead from the Canadian High Commission the decision to leave was easy.

We spent eighteen months in New Zealand and during the time we had there we can all say it was a great experience and we are glad that we did the journey. We had made friends with some great people and we were sad to wave goodbye to them and a home that we had wanted so much. The biggest task we had in front of us was to inform our family and friends back home and to enjoy the last few months we had left in Kiwi land.

Christmas had arrived and we were packed and ready to meet Lance's sister and family in Rotorua. As we were leaving New Zealand we wanted to make sure we would see all of those places both on the North Island and the South Island that we wanted to see whilst we were there. One of the places being Rotorua and as it was also a place of interest for Lance's sister and family it was a good destination to meet up after fourteen months of not seeing each other. With all the greetings, hugs and kisses done it was time to hit the shops to buy food and drink to celebrate their arrival and of course that festive time of year. The evening went with a bang, many laughs and jokes accompanied by many bottles of bubbly and a good mixture of red and white wine was consumed. Always a recipe for disaster to mix drinks like that but at the time nobody cared, I should have done!

In the morning the realisation of the amount of alcohol we had consumed hit me and to be polite I felt rather worse for wear. In fact I felt that bad I thought I needed hospital treatment for alcohol poisoning. To top it off we were going to drive for a couple of hours to see Huka falls and Craters of the Moon near Taupo. Not to be, I was so poorly on the journey I could not cope so along with my closest friend bucket we turned back! Once my raging hangover had finished after some extra strength mushroom soup made by Lance, you know the condensed soup that you add water too, yes that but with no water added! It filled my empty stomach and did help enormously and after a rest I felt much more human than I had done several hours earlier.

The previous nights motel, across the road from the one we had booked for the second night was bluntly awful. It had been recently taken over and the place was in a poor state of affairs, dirty and not pleasant at all. Hence why we did not intend to stay the second night as booked and luckily we all managed to find a suitable room in the motel across the road that in comparison was a palace.

We spent a second day at Rotorua having a look around and unfortunately getting caught up in the mass floods the place had while we were there. It was that bad the road to our motel was cut off and in the town people had actually been washed away but thankfully they had been found a few hours later rather shaken but un-harmed. We had seen the sights we wanted to see in Rotorua so it was time to go home.

I have mentioned in the book that New Zealand has some of the worst roads if you suffer from travel sickness; they are that bad that the roads could make the most strongest stomachs grumble. The journey back from Rotorua is a winding one and inevitably the bucket we named Huey was well used. Travelling anywhere from Gisborne was just such a task and that really did not help the isolated feeling. There is nothing worse than dreading a trip when you know what you will have to endure during it. It makes the journey completely un-enjoyable and predictable. We had agreed with Lance's sister to make our own way back to Gisborne as they wanted to stop off at a couple of places on the way, places that we had seen numerous times so for us it was a straight journey back home.

Our house was not should I say huge, it was comfortable and suited us well. It was certainly not big enough to accommodate another five people so our guests had arranged to stay at one of the local campgrounds near the beach that had some not bad two-bedroom units. Lance had arranged that for their second week they could stay in one of the hospital flats just like the ones we had stayed in. That was totally against the hospital protocol but the guy who dealt with the accommodations had been really good to us in the past and had basically told a few white lies. He had said that it was us that needed the accommodation in order to secure a flat for our visitors. He could have been in serious trouble if he had been found out and it would have been very likely that he would of lost his job so he was taking quite a risk to help us out. That did not go un-recognised and he was rewarded with a big thank you and a few bottles of beer.

Time flies when you are having fun and we enjoyed having the company. Christmas is quite lonely when you have no friends and family to share it with so after our first lonely non-festive feeling Christmas the year before it was a very welcome change. The weather was still hard to get used to for us British folk who are used to cold chilly Christmases. Summer does not quite go with Christmas and it does most definitely take some of the jolliness away from the whole period. That was our opinion anyway and not the opinion of all immigrants who come from a country where the seasons are the other way around as some can adapt easily and are not bothered by it but it was a tough time for us.

Christmas Day 2006 was a day to remember, not just because it was a family affair but also because it was to be our last Christmas in New Zealand. We had received our letter from the Canadian High Commission a few weeks before Lance's sister had arrived requesting that we arrange our medicals. We knew from our medicals in 2005 for New Zealand that we were all healthy and that letter was merely the final piece of our emigration to Canada jigsaw, we had it in the bag so to speak! That was one of the best Christmas presents we could have asked for and so with a few weeks to go before Christmas we booked our medicals for January in Auckland. We could enjoy Christmas knowing that we had almost finished a very long tough process. However we had been led to believe that the medicals were not a walk in the park and quite invasive and very thorough so we did have slight concerns over that.

Whilst we were in New Zealand we had talked many a time about going over "The Ditch" as it is called over there and it means the short strip of ocean to Australia. It would have been silly not to have gone when we were so close and with the definite notion we were leaving New Zealand a trip to OZ was a must. We therefore booked a two-week holiday for February 2007 to travel from Brisbane up to Cairns, the Sunshine Coast in a motor home. The big motivator for that particular area of Australia was the Great Barrier Reef, the Whitsunday's and of course the famous Zoo in Beerwah that was owned by a well known and well missed conservationist. I had long grown out of the childhood excitement phase of visiting a zoo but the thought of that particular zoo brought those feelings back. With the holiday in Australia booked along with the medicals we could sit back and relax in relative comfort.

A few weeks prior to our visitors arriving I had undertaken a marathon baking session and made plenty of cakes, mince pies and festive muffins to fill the freezer and to provide some cheaper home cooked fare that in my opinion is much better for you and tastier than shop bought products.

Christmas Day had arrived and the shared cooking had been arranged so we all knew what we were doing or rather what the head women were doing! I was in charge of the baked ham and some of the trimmings whilst Lance's sister Vickie was to cook the over sized chicken and some vegetables. Cooking for ten was no small challenge and as I take pride in my cooking (Others say I am a perfectionist) I felt slightly under pressure to achieve the best and tastiest part of my menu. I do not want to sing my own trumpet here but I did as usual a very good job and the ham was delicious, the chicken and vegetables were equally as good and between the two of us we managed to cook up a true festive feast. The pudding was a simple Pavlova of fresh fruit and cream. Apparently and do not hold me to this the Pavlova is New Zealand's famous pudding and was thought up in New Zealand many moons ago despite the calls of success of the pudding from the folk from Australia. In fact the origin of the Pavlova actually featured in a long running advert in New Zealand so it is quite a serious matter between the two countries.

With the dinner finished and with the usual bloated I cannot move a muscle feeling the dreaded washing of all the many dishes was to hand. Luckily for the two chefs we had been reprieved at the last minute and the task of washing up was handed to the others. We had been stood up cooking for most of the day so we well deserved to put our feet up and take it easy, letting the monstrous dinner land properly.

I have always wondered why each Christmas we eat and drink until we feel ill, then say we will not do that next year, to then go and do it again the next year and for that matter every year. Do we not learn I ask myself?

The days that followed Christmas day were spent getting over the big meal and of course eating the leftovers that we all have after cooking too much, another lesson we never learn, do not buy too much food!

Once Christmas Day was over and done with, Lance's sister's departure day was coming around fast. New Year was a few days away and the 4th January fly back to the UK date was now not in the distance as it was a few weeks before. The weather had been glorious the whole time unlike the month of February when my Dad had visited in 2006.

New Year was to be a low-key affair really; it is not wise to drink too much when a long haul flight is only a few days away. It can also be said that after putting a few away over the festive days prior drinking a glass of wine seems a lot of trouble and in our case the wine was replaced by a cup of hot tea or two. My home baking had slowly depleted and the unusual chocolate zucchini cake had been a huge hit, it did not as first thought taste much of vegetables so I will most definitely make them for the following Christmases to come. Courgette plants can yield a huge abundance of fruit and cooking them in the usual way of roasting and stuffing can get boring so making a cake out of them is a different but a tasty change and a healthier option.

With all the food and drink mostly gone and with the New Year of 2007 welcomed in it was time to say goodbye for now to our guests. We had arranged to visit the UK for the month of May after our Australia trip in February and our South Island tour that we had booked for April, once we had sold Waiteata Street and packed our belongings and sent them on the way to Canada. We hoped, we would be free to enjoy our last holiday in New Zealand. We had packed a lot of travelling into those last months and along with arranging the move we had taken an awful lot on.

It was as hard as we thought for both sides to say goodbye as we had enjoyed a really good couple of weeks. Both spending time together visiting local attractions and of course Lance's sister and family going their own way to explore the region as much as they could. We had all spent the majority of the time enjoying every moment and it is a period of time we will look back on with fond memories and remember our very last New Zealand Christmas.

The real hard task of getting everything ready for the big move to Canada was now upon us and we had lots to do. However it was not new to us and we were not too bothered about the few weeks ahead that would require some serious organising and time management.

The main thing and the biggest worry for us was to get out of the way our medicals at the end of January in Auckland and to indeed pass them with flying colours. Everything that we had wished for over the past few years rested on that doctor finding us in good health and of course the blood tests and x-rays coming back clear. If one of us were to fail it was all over, our Canadian dream would be finished. We were having memory flashbacks of the New Zealand medical in the UK where the doctor found Elijah had a heart murmur, it was after a private hospital consultation found to be innocent, but it did require further tests and if it were to surface again it would really hold things up. One thing we had learnt over the few years leading up to the moment of being called for the Canadian Medicals is that the Canadian High Commission is not soft. They will only accept the best possible people to enter their country and we had been fore-warned that a small medical find could spell disaster so we did feel some anxiety leading up to the medicals.

Timing was critical and everything over the months that followed Christmas and right up until the very last day we had in New Zealand was planned meticulously. We had placed all our faith in the fact that our medicals would be clear, we had booked holidays and the biggest asset to us, our house, was due to go on the market the first week of February. We had no fall back plan, which some may find rather stupid so we had to pass those medicals or our future would be a very uncertain one.

The big day arrived; we had travelled up to Auckland the day before the medicals were due to take place. Gisborne to Auckland is a full days drive and we wanted to arrive at the surgery reasonably relaxed if that was possible under the circumstances!

We waited in the sitting area of that surgery for about half an hour and I can tell you that it was like waiting for the worst moment of your life to come. The tension was just too much and at times the idea of running seemed a very easy option but that would not have helped our Canadian emigration in the slightest. All we could do was to sit tight and twiddle those very nervous thumbs and await our personal interrogation!

I have to be completely honest with what I am about to write. I have stated in this book that I shall only give you the truth that I can give on our personal experiences. The following is in no way I am sure the usual medical examination practice for prospective Canadian Immigrants but our experience was not at all what we expected. A visit with our own GP would have been more invasive and the hardest part of the whole medical was the walk to the blood collecting centre and local x-ray department and the huge task of trying to find a taxi to get back to the surgery to give them our x-rays. It was the most easiest medical we have ever endured, the New Zealand medical we had in 2005 was in our opinion quite tough in comparison to the Canadian one and that was not that bad. We were in the room with the doctor for less than ten minutes and he asked three questions of which were based on the usual, "Do you smoke or drink and how much if you do?" We were weighed and our height measured and that was really and honestly it! No prodding in the more sensitive areas that we were told would be examined and no tricky embarrassing questions asked, just a questionnaire to fill in prior to the appointment. It was a huge relief I can tell you and completely mind boggling to say the least as we had expected to be really dragged over the coals, it was a walk in the park.

I know that if we had undergone the medical in the UK it would have been much more thorough as I had talked to a surgery about the medical examinations before we submitted our permanent residence application back in November 2004. For that particular surgery we would have been there all day, prodded and poked and attached to a heart monitor whilst exercising, so we got off very lightly in New Zealand. The experience we had in Auckland does not mean all Canadian medial examinations would be so simple and easy. Different countries have different views on what a medical involves however I am sure that all panel doctors must have set guidelines to follow, how thorough they are is up to them.

It is against the rules for the doctor to disclose your medical results to you but in our case the doctor was quite open in telling us everything was fine and we should not have anything to worry about, we were all in good working order.

With all that done and the paperwork sent off we could relax and enjoy our next holiday, two weeks in Australia in a motor home. The Sunshine Coast was our pick up destination.

From Kiwi to Kangaroo

Australia was a holiday destination that I had never really thought about too much. I suppose the main reason being the ones I have already mentioned, the deadly animals. However when I was younger and watched the Australian soaps I always wished I could be there as well.

We would have been rather silly not to visit whilst we were so close so the decision was made to give it a go, all be it slightly hesitant on my behalf. Looking back on it now I can't understand why I was so worried as I knew people from work back in the UK who had spent quite some time in Australia and had never seen hide nor hair of any deadly creatures. It was hardly like they were swarming everywhere like I imagined.

We touched down in Brisbane at the beginning of February 2007 for the start of our two-week holiday. Unlike the Canadian motor home company we were not required to spend the night in a hotel prior to picking up the motor home so we went straight from the airport. Ironically we were the first people to have that motor home as it was brand new and the only journey it had made was from the dealer to the hire company. Our Canadian motor home was also brand new!

After the usual talk and explanation from the staff we were free to go but the motor home was not automatic and it was tricky to drive. Lance took the helm and we were soon on our way in search of the nearest supermarket to stock the cupboards up with food. Much easier said than done, finding the supermarket was not that hard but the parking was difficult and the car park was very tight for such a big vehicle, it was all becoming very familiar!

With the shopping done and the food unpacked we headed out of the shopping centre car park and towards the highway. Unfortunately there was a diversion on the road and a simple trip to the highway turned into a lost mission in the suburbs of Brisbane. The stress levels crept up and we were soon very anxious. As usual I could not read the street map for love nor money and I did not have a clue where we were on it. In the end Lance had to pull up and go and knock on a house to find out if they could direct us on the right road that would lead us out of the place. Australians are honest people and say exactly what they are thinking; they are as the saying goes ("fair dinkum") telling you as it is and a trait that we admired by the end of our holiday. At that precise moment though being told that I was a hopeless map-reader and should be given the sack was a hurtful criticism off a stranger, although it was very true.

Eventually we found the highway and headed north. Our first stop was to be near Beerwah but the maps we had been given by the company were pretty hopeless and we soon found finding a campsite was not easy. For the second time that day the stress levels peaked and we ended up stopping at a service station come information centre to ask for some decent maps. We were given a huge pile of maps and guides but they were also pretty useless in providing any information about where we could stay so we had to make best of what we had.

The highway was an easy drive, very straight and we soon reached the Glass House Mountains. Beerwah was not too far from there along the newly named Steve Irwin Way. We took a slight detour off the main road onto a side route that would also take us to Beerwah and up to the recreation area over looking the Glass House Mountains. It was a nice place, definitely Australian in everyway. The rain was quite heavy but the advantage was the rain stopped the mosquitoes from biting and we did not mind that at all. It is hard to believe that a place could look so wild and rugged yet so beautiful and what we saw in front of us was both. We could not imagine how all of the scientists and conservationists that study such areas come out of those remote places in tact, but I can understand what draws them to such terrain.

It was at that first stop into the wilds that we came across our first true Australian, well two in fact and I did not like either. The toilet block was home to a huge Golden Orb Spider and when I say huge I mean huge, it was as big as a dinner plate with its legs of course. Lance is not too afraid of spiders and will catch and pick up the most grotesque of the house variety, however on that occasion he was not so keen to become too familiar with that type of arachnid and opted to poke the web with a long stick. The stick poking did not last too long after I pointed out that the spider may actually come down the stick rather quicker than he could possibly react in annoyance to the intruder so after a few pictures we left it be. Our inquisitive side took hold of us at that point and we walked around the toilet block seeing what else we could find. It was not too long before we found another spider but that time definitely no poking, it was as you can probably guess a red back, small yes, pretty yes, well sort of, dangerous yes! We had heard prior to the trip that they like toilets so it was not too much of a surprise that we saw the red back at that location but it was our first day in Australia and seeing them so soon was not expected.

Excitement of our nature forage over, we climbed back into the motor home and followed the road to Beerwah and a sign-post for a local campsite. Luck is never kind to us with regards to first day holiday accommodation and that day was no exception. The signpost lead us to nowhere that we could see a camp-site and for the third time that day we started to get rather agitated. It was getting late and the light was fading fast so it was imperative that we found somewhere sharpish to pull up and have a bite to eat and chill out. Unbeknown to us at the time we had actually been going the right way and if we had gone two more kilometres along the road we would have ended up at the front door of the campsite. We had turned around and spent an extra stressful half hour going round in a circle! Finally we managed to locate the site and with only two spaces available we were just in time. Why we have such first night bad luck I do not know.

That night I did not sleep too well, one because the motor home was on a slight angle and secondly I was anxiously look-ing forward to the following days expedition to the famous zoo. Since the owner of the zoo had died in a freak accident with a stingray I had taken some interest in his life and found the whole thing quite distressing. I was anxious as I knew the zoo would be full of reminders of its famous owner who's life was cut so sadly short, the thought of crying like a baby had crossed my mind and it was not something I hoped would happen.

We arrived reasonably early to take full advantage of the zoo, as it was not likely that we would be visiting again in the near future so we had a day to make the most of it. The tragedy was still fresh as it had only happened about four months prior and the zoo had not as yet changed the images that confront you as you enter. The big and bold images of a man and his family so happy in their being, it was very sad to see.

I will not bore you with a written tour of the zoo as it would not do the place justice but I can tell you that it is a place everyone must visit at some point in his or her lives.

Despite my fears I did not have any crying episodes as such despite the feeling of sadness in a few areas of the zoo. The area where the famous shows were filmed was poignant as the show opened with few words being spoken and the famous phrase "Crikey" being shouted in honour of the great man. It was certainly a heartfelt moment shared by many I am certain and my shades spent some time on during that show to hide my bleary eyes.

The area behind the crocoseum was the location of the many tributes, signed shirts and letters of sadness and it was an area that I could not bring myself to go to as it would have definitely set of the water works and I did not want to walk around the zoo with panda eyes.

The animals were amazing, the enclosures the animals were kept in were more than satisfactory, and it showed a true dedication to all the occupants. It was with no question of a doubt the best zoo I have ever been to and I cannot imagine a zoo in the world that could match it in anyway, it was truly amazing.

From Beerwah we headed north on the M1 highway. We did not have any set plans on where to stop as such as we knew two weeks to complete such a distance would be tricky and most days would encompass quite a few hours of driving. In hindsight I wish we could have booked more time but that would have been impossible due to Lance's employment and financially not agreeable. Despite that we had some ideas of what we would like to see but in reality we found the distance of the highway to some of those places was the equivalent of an extra days drive there and back and we just did not have the time to make those journeys. We stuck mainly to the highway and spent the nights at the free campsites that were frequent along the way.

The Sunshine Coast is littered with beaches but unfortunately those beaches were like I say not close to the highway so we missed out on a lot of nice locations on the coast along the way. It was a huge disappointment for us but unavoidable when you are tied to such a short schedule. There were a few locations further up towards Bowen that we would definitely try to see though if we could.

I cannot really say too much about the flora and fauna that we saw that first week as to be honest we spent little time away from the main highway. All we noticed was the impeccably straight long roads and the red earth. We saw many signs for koala's and kangaroos but never sighted any, as it was hard to see anything whilst whizzing along at the speed limit. We did stop a few times for the usual side of the road relieve oneself in the bushes and we did come across some rather un-friendly purple ants that you would most definitely not want in your pants! We did see some odd-looking stick insects and cicadas at one camp and some very green tree frogs finding their home for the night in the toilet. Other than that the wildlife kept pretty well hidden from us.

The heat was not too bad the first week but as we got further north we started getting the humidity of the rainforest and it was honestly like being in a tumble dryer all the time. The air con would not suffice so we would open the window to let in a nice cool breeze only to find you were belted with hot air that did not cool us down. All of our clothes just clung to us damp all the time, it was not too pleasant but we coped and enjoyed the experience, sort of!

We had intended to stop at Bundaberg where I am sure some of you will know is the location where the famous ginger beer is made but it was indeed a huge drive away and not for the first time we had to abort the idea. The whole holiday could be sounding very boring but I can assure you we did have some fun and games and there is one occasion that we can still recall quite clearly today and I will elaborate on that in the pages to come. On our travels we stopped for the night at a place called Gin Gin, famous for its pies and of course as pie connoisseurs we could not resist! The pies did not receive any criticism from us and that is quite an honour as we usually find fault in most of the pies we try!

Anyway to get the story back on track we came across an old couple in a very nice bus type motor home and chatted to them for a while. They had long retired and actually lived their lives on the Gold Coast in between touring Australia in their mobile home, a journey that they actually did regularly. Spending more time travelling than they spent at home and who can blame them? It turned out that he was a keen fisherman just like us and told us of a few secret locations to fish for barramundi. We had spent a bit of money buying a new fishing rod, two to be exact, bait and all the necessities to catch a fish and up until that moment in time we had not even got them out of the pack. So it was music to our ears and we planned to fish at the Monduran Dam the next day and hopefully catch a nice big barramundi to throw in the frying pan.

Now if you have learnt anything during this book you will have learnt that our fishing expeditions don't quite go as planned, the plan being that a fish or two are caught. I would be lying to say that we did not catch a thing as we did or rather Lance did. He caught a not bad sized croaking catfish. Croaking to be put back in the water and because we did not know if it was edible or not we obliged and threw the flapping complaining fish back. It must have told any barramundi or any other inhabitants of the finned kind in the area to stay well clear of odd looking bits of worms floating by and we did not have one single bite after that, what a surprise!

With yet again hurt egos and fishless we headed back to the motor home and hastily made our way to the next supposed barramundi fishing spot next to the river at a place called Calliope. It was a hard place to find but we were very glad we did as it was a lovely free camp with quiet private secluded spots along the river to stop and we chose a good one. That good you could have almost cast your line into the river from the window, perfect for us and with the evidence of fish scales everywhere obviously a good catching spot. Without delay we baited up and whilst Lance was making a cuppa and the kids splashed their stick rods in the water I cast out. Just for the record here is another example of how our fishing capers do not go as planned! We had bought two rods, one with good strong line and one with line that I doubted would be strong enough to land a fish of smallish proportions. Again you can guess what happened, almost instantly the small inadequate rod hooked up with what I could only guess was a large barramundi! A large barramundi that once it realised it was hooked went off like a steam train. I have never had the opportunity to hook up to one before but I believed from fishing shows that they fought hard. Fight hard it did, a one-way fight really as my line was totally useless against such a weight and after only two minutes at the most of screaming up the river the line gave up.

Sometimes I wonder why we bother to fish at all, we must be the only people in the world that have such bad luck when it comes to a good fishing trip. We have spent so much money on tackle, rods and fuel to get to the places that in relation we could have probably bought tons of fish from the fishmongers and saved a whole heap of money. I try to tell myself and Lance whom waivers all the time that a big one may be lurking for us. In that case it was but lurking on the wrong rod! Those of you who are fellow anglers know that when you lose a fish especially a good one it is the most aggravating, gut churning feeling you can experience, let alone down right inconvenient but we all still fish, as there is always hope. My hope had run out the minute my line snapped and despite our failing bait which had by then gone horrible we persevered relentlessly. At least the children were enjoying themselves at the waters edge, pretending to fish with a long stick, a piece of line that we had tied on and a leaf for bait. The weather was fine and we could not have asked for a better location, sitting at the waters edge watching the sun slowly slip down behind the clouds.

As dark was falling we noticed a couple of boys throwing a small net into the shallows to catch small fish obviously for barra bait, we could not quite understand why they were shining their torches across the river, maybe to attract the fish to the light at a guess. The next morning it all became perfectly clear. I have to mention now that throughout the previous week we had been joking about crocodiles and the possibility of coming across one being rather remote and we had even joked at the rivers edge whilst fishing in the murky river and watching the children play in the shallows. So it came as a bit of a shock when

Josh came running back shouting look at the sign, a sign less than a few meters away from where we were camping. It was a big yellow sign warning all persons that estuarine crocodiles inhabited the area. Next to that sign was another telling all persons to be aware that stingers (toxic jellyfish) inhabited the area also. We could not believe our eyes as we felt we had been so negligent. I have watched many wildlife programs were crocodile's power out of the water and grab unsuspecting wildebeest in a split second. The thought that we could have been croc food or more to the point that one of the children could have been taken hit us and from that point on we would take more care and think about where we were a bit more. The shock did not dampen our spirits too much and we did fish for a short while the next morning, that time though the children stayed well away from the water and we fished from a few meters back. The fish were not too interested apart from a medium size bream that I caught, big enough for the pan and a meal for one. Calliope was more of a fishing spot than we had initially thought and as the morning went on more and more fishermen turned up, it was becoming crowded so we thought it best to continue our journey.

Calliope had one last shock up its sleeve. We observed an old couple fishing not from the shore but from the top of the bridge that went over the river. The gentleman seemed to struggle to cast out, and it seemed rather strange to us until we realised he had a completely false arm. He could have only been a local, fished there regularly I would have thought but why was he fishing from a high vantage point and more to the point what had happened to his arm! It could appear to the more suspicious of people that the Calliope adventure was over exaggerated but I can honestly tell you that it is all completely true. The kids were splashing and banging at the waters edge and we did see a guy with a false arm. We could have had a croc a few meters away and we would not have known a thing. A very important lesson that we learned is do not joke about things as serious as crocodiles in places where your joke may well turn into your worst nightmare.

Once we left Calliope we continued to make good headway to Rockhampton, the beef capital of Australia. A point that they are obviously very proud of as the city has several statues of bulls dotted around in full view. Rockhampton also lies on the Tropic of Capricorn and at the tourist information site just as you come into the city there is a monument to that. We did not do it but there is a web cam located at the I-Site and if you stand in front of it and let a family member or friend know by phone they can look at the website and see you.

For the couple of days prior we had made quite good time and did not have to rush through Rockhampton without seeing some of the tourist attractions. The zoo was worth a look or that was what we had been told anyway so why not take a look, we thought. After the best zoo in Australia how could a city zoo fair, well not good. The poor animals, those that they had lived in poorly maintained enclosures and had little room, the saying "You can't swing a cat" springs to mind. I suppose it is just a city zoo's tale of poor funding but it was sad to see after observing animals living in such luxury in comparison a few days earlier. I think my disgust must have been passed on to one of the many Ibis birds that flocked on the trees as one decided to relieve itself on my head, my shoulder and my handbag, it was to say the least disgusting and for a large bird a rather large effort. Along with my new hair colour and the many big mosquitoes that had been following us we thought it best that I clean up as good as I could and depart the sorry place. For those people who have not had a taste of the country or witnessed animals in a setting not too different from the wild a city zoo must be the best thing since sliced bread and I suppose a city zoo has its place to teach those the ins and outs of an animal's life. However it was not for us and after a quick shop at the local store we carried on north towards our halfway point of Mackay.

We had been forewarned that the stretch from Rockhampton to Mackay was boring with not much to see and the road was long and straight. We had been correctly informed, the journey was indeed boring and the road just kept on going and going and going. Regular driving shifts were undertaken to avoid driver fatigue, those moments when you are so bored that you're concentration waivers and everything starts to blend into one.

Our holiday was nearing its final week and we had made it to our halfway destination a day earlier than anticipated. A good move, as we did not want to miss seeing the Whitsunday's and the well-photographed Airlie beach. We had looked the Whitsunday's and Airlie beach up on the Internet and I can even remember seeing it on an episode of a well-known Australian soap once and it looked like paradise.

The old couple back in Gin Gin who had rightly told us about the boring stretches also told us that Airlie Beach was rather tourist orientated and spoilt because of that. They actually told us not to really bother but we decided not to take that advice and we went anyway. To our total amazement they had been absolutely right, it was so busy and totally over the top for tourists. I was so disappointed that such a small-secluded place had been taken over by money grabbers and spoilt beyond recognition I am sure from its original self. The weather did not help the overall picture; it was miserable, cold, windy and very wet. I have seen many pictures of the Whitsunday's over the years and relished in the idea of one day visiting those white sand beaches and clear blue seas. All the way from Brisbane right up until that day we had all looked forward to visiting that place, how more disappointed could we have been. The sand was horrible and dirty littered with rubbish. Crime was obviously high in the area, as the toilet roll holders in the toilets had actually been padlocked on. I have seen clearer seas back home in the UK and certainly the New Zealand beaches around Gisborne were far superior to the brown choppy soup that was in front of us. I could not imagine anyone wishing to swim in it but Josh had a paddle up to his knees in the safety net area as the waters around there are well known for its many poisonous jellyfish. A list of them and their level of danger was listed on a sign along with a bottle of vinegar to be used if any person was stung. Personally I thought Josh was rather brave to go into water that he could not see a centimetre into despite the safety net as I would have been extremely wary of what was around my feet. I am not at all comfortable with the ocean and what lurks in it so in the most of un-threatening seas I rarely go beyond ankle level and that is pushing it. All in all I think we spent about an hour if that at Airlie beach, it was just not inspiring. However in its defence the area had experienced some heavy rain and winds so I can only assume in mid summer the place comes into its own and we had just visited at a bad time.

Next stop for us was the Peter Faust Dam. It was located a little inland, on the map anyway but in reality it was a long drive and a complete waste of fuel. Our intent was to stay at the campsite there and have a fish but on arrival we saw that the campsite was terribly run down and the reservoir was un-fish-able due to green algae that is toxic. Looking back we have done that same stupid thing many times before, taking an unplanned detour that we had not decided on prior and regretted it, we still do it now!

Trips into nowhere cost time and money let alone causing much annoyance so we turned around almost instantly and headed on the main road to Edgecombe Bay just below Bowen. We did not have to take a detour off the main road to Edge-combe Bay as it runs parallel to the main road so we could clearly see that it was not worth a stop, again brown soup.

We stayed at many camps along the way, mostly free ones, some had showers some did not. The past few nights had been spent at sites with no showers so we were glad to come across a small out of the way site at Ayr. Out of all the campsites we stayed at that one had a real outback feel to it, rough land with red soil and huge ants nests. The surrounding marshland was home to many birds and Lance and the children were lucky to witness a group of red kangaroo's, one with a baby racing through the field on the outskirts of the camp. That night it absolutely poured down, it rained that much we thought we would be flooded out. The rainy season in the north of Australia was aptly named the rainy season for a very good reason.

It seemed at that moment that we had gone to Australia to see no sights, to see no nice beaches and to spend most of the time driving on the main road looking at nothing particularly inspirational. I think we felt that way because it was partly true, we had grossly misjudged the time needed to do the Brisbane to Cairns trip and we certainly suffered for our naivety and lack of prior planning. We could not change it or do anything about it so with time ticking away and the days going by we continued on our super whistle stop tour further up into the north and true rainforest country. The humidity was really noticeable once we had reached Mackay and I had to say that to live there you would have to like heat and humid conditions.

We pushed on and made our way past Townsville and Ingham towards Tully. Tully is famous for its high rainfall and boasts a huge Wellington boot in honour of that record. A big green Wellington boot with a frog on the side that you can enter and have your photograph taken at the top if you so wished. Ironically it had been pouring down just before we arrived and started to rain again just as we left. Just past Tully was to be our next beach stop at Mission Beach, again a well-known beach to those who search the world for the best of the best. It was to us not at all the best of the best but probably the worst of the worst, it was not at all worth getting out of the motor home for. The beach was home to many small crabs that were very good at art and design; they had in their efforts to build a sand home created great artwork with little balls of sand that they scattered seemingly in a well thought out pattern. It is crazy that we visited a supposed glorious beach in Australia and found sand crabs more exiting and interesting! Maybe the recent bad weather was to blame for the lack of beauty at that time at that second beach venue. To make the point Lance had his photograph taken whilst holding a magazine with the picture of that exact beach in the summer months and what a difference it was.

As mentioned earlier we had now been driving deep into the rainforest and we came across some rather amusing signs along the way warning drivers to be aware of cassowary birds, those big emu like birds that would damage your vehicle if you happened to hit one. The warning sign was yellow and consisted of a car with its front crunched in and a rather sorry looking cassowary about to keel over, it was a comical picture but like Australians to the point.

Our holiday was coming to an end and we only had two more days left before we had to drop the motor home of at the Cairns depot and catch our flights back to New Zealand. I will again go back to the old couple in Gin Gin who gave us a wealth of advice on where to go and where not to go. Although sometimes we did not heed that advice and regretted it more often than not, a lesson learnt is to take notice of what the locals tell you. The friendly old couple also told us of a small place called Kuranda located just above Cairns and slightly inland. There was a quaint old-fashioned train station that had not been modernised and it maintained all the character of an early nineteenth century train station and was well worth a look.

We decided to take a slight detour from the main highway and take a round trip on Highway 25 that would eventually take us to Kuranda and within easy driving distance of Cairns for our last day. It has to be said it was the only worthwhile detour that we took during the whole holiday and the road took us towards a small town called Tarzali. We had read in a brochure that there was a small fishing company there were you could catch Jade perch (a fish well known for its high omega content) and buy crayfish so we thought it would be a good idea to have a go and hopefully have better luck than we had encountered over the past two weeks previous.

It was late afternoon by that time and we planned the fishing trip for the next day so we set about looking for the local campsite that was on the map. Just before we reached Tarzali we came across a free forest campsite that at first glance looked very nice, it was quiet and very much located in the rainforest. It was also totally empty and as we like peace and quiet a perfect spot for the night. We chose a pitch not too hidden just in case of an emergency and with all the good intentions of staying for the night we arranged the sleeping lay out. After a brisk stroll to the local hole in the ground, the middle of nowhere style toilet block we thought it would be an adventure to follow a small track into the forest and see what we could see. As in most areas accessible for walking a sign was strategically placed at the beginning of the track to inform all what to look out for along the way. It is hard to believe that there was a swimming hole located somewhere amongst the dense rainforest and more to the point in our opinion you would have to be a sandwich short of a picnic to go swimming in a water hole in the middle of the Australian rainforest with all the creatures that could be in there to join you. I am sure that there are plenty of adventurous individuals out there who would relish that idea but not us.

The rainforest was living up to its name, it was very wet but with a dose of what I can now assume was bravery we acknowledged the stinging plant warning and with hands in pockets and strict instructions for the children to keep them there we slowly and cautiously made our way along the narrow path. Stinging plants are in no way like the stinging nettles we are used to in the UK. Oh no the Australian plants are poisonous, heart shaped leaves with hairs that if brushed against can penetrate the skin causing immense pain for months. It was wilder than we had first thought but the sign also mentioned the possibility of maybe seeing a platypus in the water so we continued along with pounding hearts and finally reached the viewing platform. Platform was not the right description at all; a slippery slope that Lance nearly skidded feet first down was a better description. It was all starting to feel at bit too much and the thought of what lay in the undergrowth was taking an irrational hold on us both and so we dithered about for a few moments trying to decide whether or not to continue. It was then that the forest decided for us as a huge tree came crashing down less than two meters away and that was enough to send us on our heels back to the motor home. Lance nearly slipping and plunging into the unknown along with a tree nearly landing on our heads was like the rainforests way of asking us to leave and that is exactly what we did. Snakes, stinging plants, spiders and all things dangerous had completely taken over our minds and with the distinct lack of other campers we did not feel too safe. It was time to find the original campsite we had chosen before stumbling onto the more rough and ready version and with little will to hang around we did indeed beat a hasty retreat.

Not too far from the wild campsite and literally just before reaching our destination of Tarzali we took a small circuit road off the main route that went past three waterfalls. The detour took all of fifteen minutes and was worth the added time. The waterfalls came in the order of Millaa Millaa, Zillia and last Elinjaa but the order does depend on which way around you take the circuit! Elinjaa falls was a good choice of name in our view and for obvious reasons; Elijah found it amusing to have a waterfall called after him, which is what we told him anyway. We did only glimpse Elinjaa falls from a distance as it was a slight walk down some rather precarious looking steps and the last thing we wanted to do at that moment was to take another excursion into the forest so we let it be and with the knowledge that we had seen the best of the waterfalls prior we did not mind at all.

We finally found the campsite and although it was expensive we were all tired and hungry, just wanting to settle down for the evening. Our timing could not have been better and we connected the camper up to the electric and water station outside a few minutes before the heavens opened. Our evening entertainment was to watch the late arrivals struggle against the torrential rain and gale force winds in an attempt to have power and fresh water. We shouldn't have laughed at their expense but after our eventful day we needed to have a giggle and it alleviated our anxiety. The campsite had some amazing photographs of the damage that was caused when Hurricane Larry battered that area and the rest of Tropical Northern Queensland in 2006, it must have been a terrifying ordeal to witness such brute power.

The next morning did not bring any better weather and the sky was still heavy with rain but in the Baird spirit of things we still planned on fishing at the local fisheries further up the road. After a swift breakfast and tidy we left our rain sodden pitch and pulled into the fishery with good intentions to fish. Unfortunately by the time we arrived the weather had decided to once again pour down and we could not fish in such conditions as we would have all been soaking wet within minutes so instead we opted to buy some fresh fish and cray's for our evening meal. The fish could not have been any fresher as the guy netted them out of a tank, quickly dispatched them and prepared them for us.

The owner was another true example of a pure Australian, he was a nice chap who had suffered greatly from the devastating tornado, in fact he had lost everything and he had little choice but to sell the business and move on. It was a sad tale of a once thriving business. He had invested a great deal of money in new equipment and structural changes to his shop months before the tornado struck and it destroyed it all, thousands and thousands of dollars worth of hard work was taken in minutes. The location was lovely and both Lance and I would have sincerely loved to have bought that fisheries but it was way out of our reach, both in asking price and in the amount of money needed on top to re-build it. It was just such a great place but only a very wealthy person would of benefited in buying the business and so with fish and cray's in tow we headed out of Tarzali and onward to our final sightseeing destination of Kuranda.

The areas that I have mentioned in Northern Tropical Queensland fall into a region called the Atherton Tablelands, it is home to World Heritage listed sights such as, lakes, rivers, waterfalls, magnificent rainforests and National Parks, a beautiful must see location and highly recommended.

On route to Kuranda we stopped to look at one last waterfall, Malanda Falls. The area in front of the falls itself was a swimming pool but with murky brown water. I could not envisage anyone venturing into the unknown, however I am sure that some people would be less weedy than I and take the plunge anyway.

Kuranda train station was as quaint as the old couple that had told us about it but it was a small little town and the station was the only thing we had an interest in. It was hard to navigate a large motor home around those small streets and we had gained valuable experience of small places and large vehicles whilst in Canada in 2005 so we knew when we should call it a day and not tempt fate. After a walk around the train station and down to the river and back we took some pictures of the place and decided it would be a good idea to drive to our final campsite of our holiday, Lake Placid just outside of Cairns, no not the famous Lake Placid with the giant crocodile just a namesake but funny anyway.

Back on the main road we discovered the roadside and fields were covered with huge red termite mounds, some must have been two or more meters high and quite an impressive architectural feat for such small creatures and well worth a photograph or two. It is really unbelievable what insects can construct; they do not attend college to learn those skills, it is remarkable.

Our plan for the final night was to stay as close to Cairns as possible without actually being on top of the place. So to our joy we noticed in a brochure that there was such a campsite. Close enough for a leisurely drive into Cairns to drop the motor home off but a nice distance away also. Yes we did also think it was namesake to the movie and wondered if the lake was infested with giant man eating crocodiles fed by a little old lady!

Finding Lake Placid turned out to be quite a challenge as the map did not quite correspond with where it actually was, it was not on that occasion my poor map reading skills but rather bad map coordinates. After a tense half an hour wondering if we had driven past it we came across the campsite sign and followed the road directly to the lake. We had paid to stay at some mediocre places along the way as we had little choice but more often than not we stayed at the free campsites. The higher up toward Cairns we got the free camps got fewer and far between so we were forced to opt for what we could find and they were not always the best. However in the case of Lake Placid we could not have asked for a nicer paid campsite, it was in a beautiful location with the lake situated in front and a bar come restaurant situated next door in the rainforest. The site was tidy and clean and sported a lovely outdoor heated pool that we intended to make full use of after washing and drying our laundry and packing the suitcases ready for the journey home the next day. The last day of any holiday for us anyway consists of repacking and sorting all our belongings and looking through the leaflets picked up along the way. It is part of the holiday winding down time and a time to reflect on the two weeks we had spent in Australia.

The hours went by quickly and after the packing had been completed, the motor home washed and cleaned inside and out we went over to the bar for a few beers. We had heard of the deadly cane toads and that night we were lucky to witness a handful of them hopping along the road, at a distance of course! That night the rainforest was kind to us by showing us many creatures from cane toads to lizards to small and large insects of all shapes and sizes. It was a great end to our holiday and with a belly full of Australian beer and happy minds we slept our last night in Australia with the sound of the local wildlife ringing in our ears.

We awoke the next morning to the sound of the resident kookaburras and after a quick swim, shower and a last minute tidy we walked across to the restaurant for a hearty breakfast. We were not disappointed as hearty it was with more than enough food to go around which it did. We had to vacate the campsite by 10am but our flights were not until 11pm at night so we took our time in returning the motor home and had a look at a few places on the way, places like Yorkeys Knob that as you can imagine caused a snigger or two on our behalf. Places to visit for tea stops slowly ran out so it was time to return the vehicle that we had called home and catch a taxi to Cairns airport six hours before our scheduled flight. We had not been to Cairns airport before and for those readers who have they may have a smile on their faces, as they know what I am about to write! For some reason we had envisaged Cairns airport to be like many of the others we had been to, places to eat, shops to look in and generally enough to do to waste those hours away.

We were in for a huge shock, the international terminal was empty, it was more to the point deserted and the multitude of places to eat and shops to look in were well none existent! It was like a ghost town and with six hours to waste not a good find. After many circuits of the small terminal we finally came across a member of staff who informed us that the food court and shops would not open until an hour before the flight was due to depart and that food was available in the domestic terminal. So with a large luggage trolley we went over to the domestic terminal to find that it was also very small scale and to top it off to actually enter the shopping area we had to go through customs! With little option we had to pay to store our luggage and be interrogated just to get a meal. It was in our opinion way over the top but part of the process nowadays. Eventually time went slowly by and we departed Australia as scheduled in a rather old airplane that made all sorts of weird noises during take off, a little worrying don't you think?

I was glad to be going home but I wished we could have had more time in Australia. We had spent only two weeks travelling a small proportion of the country but just that small part had imprinted on us greatly and talking for us both here we left a piece of us back there at that airport. We have never really felt that attached to any other place we have visited over the last couple of years apart from Canada. Maybe we should have spent our time on the other side of the world in good old Oz instead of New Zealand but if we all could see into the future our lives would be boring and adventures would be a thing of the past. Better to experience the uncertainty and variety that life brings rather than experience a foreseen predictable one-way street.

Back to Bedlam

Upon arrival back at Waiteata Street we were pleasantly surprised to find that our open homes had been a huge hit with many viewings. We were lucky to have purchased the house at a good price for such a beautiful location within a well sort after area and we hoped for a good sale price when the hammer came down on auction day. I have to say that using the right choice of realtor and having an agent who is your friend is a good way in which to gain the best possible price. There are so many bad real estate agents out there and we nearly chose very badly but more on that later.

It was then the end of February 2007 and with little over a month to go before the house sale and we were to leave on our South Island tour we still had a lot to arrange. We had been in New Zealand for only eighteen months, a short period of time in comparison to others but we had collected numerous belongings in that time and they could not all go to Canada with us. For the second time in just over two years we were going to hold a garage sale as they call it over in New Zealand and we really hoped that it would be a bigger success than our UK flop back in 2005.

The one good aspect of Gisborne was the lack of choice when it came to the International Removal Companies as in the UK there are many and it is a task in itself to pick one suitable for your needs. We did not have such a dilemma the second time around and with only two to choose from it was not too difficult to make our minds up. I think the biggest factor for choosing the local company was saving about six thousand dollars. The larger well known companies can literally charge the earth but we were happy and the date for packing was set for the 4th April 2007, the day after the house auction.

I have always been a good organiser and I had all of our dates worked out in perfect order. We would sell the house, get our belongings packed up and leave for the two week South Island holiday and then fly back home to the UK for a planned months catch up with friends and family. In between time we would somehow sell both cars and all the belongings that we were not taking to Canada. So as you can imagine we had a fairly organised schedule but tight to say the least but I always say, "Where there is a will there is a way" a very true phrase, we can all do anything we want if we want it badly enough.

Things were falling into place and the house was getting ever increasing interest, we had good vibes that we would be very happy come auction day. On the other side of the coin we had to come to terms with a heartbreaking decision and it was not easy to realise that not everything can go the way you want. As I mentioned earlier in the book we had bought a lovely boxer puppy a few months earlier and we had all the intentions of taking Jake with us if we left (at the time of getting him our imminent Canadian move was not yet known) I started to look for a pet service that dealt with flying pets all over the world and found that the price was not too bad so it all looked good for Jake to become a Canadian boxer. It was then after speaking with the company I learned that boxers are classed in the brachycephalic breed category and that they do not cope well with long haul flights, in fact the mortality rate among those breeds is very high. They simply cannot get enough oxygen during the flight and become stressed resulting in death by asphyxiation. We could not risk getting to the other end and finding Jake had not made it so the decision was made to find him a good home. On our part it was tough, he was a nice dog and he had settled into our family well but fate played a part and we soon found him a new home with a lovely young couple that lived in Twizel, South Island. They had suffered a huge loss as their young boxer puppy was killed in a car accident some weeks earlier so it was a fitting end and Jake was a worthy replacement. Despite the happy feeling that we had located him a super home I cried buckets the day we said goodbye to him, like always Lance proved stronger and took him to the airport for his short flight to Twizel. The few days and weeks that followed seemed strange, no dog to take for a walk and no dog food in the cupboards but the couple kept in touch for a short while and sent us pictures so we could see how Jake had settled.

Auction day was nearing quickly and our garage sales had been advertised in the local paper. We inevitably had an air of worry that we would be left with perfectly good stuff to throw in the skip. A thought that was high in our minds, a negative thought embedded since the UK. Things did not go quite as planned but not in a bad way, the first sale was a huge success. We were actually not prepared for the hoards of people who turned up an hour before the sale was due to start, we were still in bed! Within an hour we had sold all of our large items, well taken deposits for them and many other smaller items, it was crazy but we could have sold some things ten times over. We could have never prepared for the deluge of people that came through the house in the first hour, literally thirty to forty people at once and all of them asking about the same things at once! I know at one point it got so bad that Lance was so close to shouting, "Get out of my house" but if he had we would have not sold what we sold. In truth it was the best sale ever, it could not have gone any better. Afterwards we needed a good few hours to redeem our senses and count up our money tin that was without surprise quite full. People warned us after the event that New Zealanders love a good bargain and that is why we had so many people turn up. We would be more prepared for the second sale and definitely be out of bed!

With regards to the Canadian High Commission we had sent back to them all that they had asked for, medicals sent from the doctor, x-rays sent from the radiology department and our final forms and photographs. The photographs needed to be a certain size for the final paperwork and not the same size as the ones that we first submitted with our original application back in 2004. The photographs also needed to be cut exactly the right size, which at first proved difficult. Most photographers leave the pictures for you to cut out and after sitting in the car in twenty-nine degrees of Gisborne sunshine and getting hotter as the minutes went by I decided to leave them for the Canadian High Commission to cut out! We could do no more as it was in the hands of the officer assigned to our file, time would tell.

Our three cats did not really cause us a concern as a neighbour had pinched two of them and they were well fed everyday on fresh meat. The main reason why they upped and left in the first place but cats are not the most loyal of creatures when it comes to their stomachs. Tammy our very loyal and last to join the family cat was as loyal as ever and needed no encouragement to stay at home, however Tammy loved the house and we hoped that the new owner would like to keep her there. She had been knocked over by a car a few weeks earlier and she had suffered a bad break in her leg that left us with two choices, to put her to sleep or to pay for the costly surgery. Putting her to sleep would have been the cheapest option but Tammy was only young and had a great character and although we did opt for that at first I could not bring myself to tell the vet to do it so surgery it was and yes it cost a fortune. We have had cats before over the years and they have never caused any real expense but the New Zealand cats thought different. Two weeks after Tammy's accident our estranged Boo cat decided to have a good fight that resulted in a huge infection on her back, she was not in our opinion our cat but in other ways she was our responsibility so off to the vets again! And yes another huge bill to sort her out and after a period of keeping her in to recuperate she ran off again! Typical. That is life I suppose and despite feeling rather annoyed at Boo for being so anti family it is how cats are and it was not her fault. There were more important things to think about at that time anyway.

We had organised everything ready for our Canadian move by mid March. We had held a second garage sale and although it was not as busy as the first sale we managed to sell the important items. The school and kindergarten had been informed that we were leaving and Lance had given his notice into work. We had taken on a huge gamble, as at that time we had not received our Canadian entry visas and although we were quietly confident we would not be refused there is always that chance. We had sold everything and the house was well into the final week of the marketing process so a refusal would have been a terrible catastrophe.

The big day finally came around with great worry and anxiety on our part. So much hard work had gone into the marketing of the house by the real estate company, our friend, and by us keeping the house tidy all the time for those open homes and last minute viewers. Was it all worth it? We had received exceptional feedback over the weeks and we knew that there would be many bidders but would the house sell for more than we wanted. We were fine up until the point when the people arrived and the auctioneer got up to commence the auction, it was one of the most nerve racking times of our lives and we sat motionless behind the curtain in the bedroom with everything crossed. The first bid stunned everyone even us as it was well above the reserve we had set, people really did want our house! The bids flew in fast and furious and within ten minutes 13 Waiteata Street had a new owner, funnily enough the lady we thought would get it did, the house had gone to another English person! She was thrilled with the house but we were more thrilled as the house had sold for an amount far beyond its level, the location and charm had done us proud.

I will skip back here to a point I made earlier regarding the choice of real estate company that we nearly made. A few weeks prior to the listing of our house a new company had moved into the city. They claimed that they could save you thousands, as you would not pay any commission, sounds good doesn't it? Well that company in particular had little if no experience in house marketing and despite our asking they could not tell us much about their companies selling successes. However money talks and the thought of saving thousand's was very appealing to us at first, so we invited an agent around to discuss selling our house through them. It soon came to light that the company left most of the hard work to the seller including arranging the open homes and deciding on the asking price. Anyway to cut a long story short we decided against them, mainly because they appeared inadequate and secondly because the agent told us that we would never reach our expected selling price. We chose wisely in the end to give our business to another new real estate company, one that did things the usual way and despite having to pay them fourteen thousand dollars in commission it was well worth it. If we had indeed stuck with the no commission company we would have lost out on more than several thousand dollars. We could have paid so dearly for thinking we would save money; we would have lost a fortune.

We had four weeks left from selling day to the day we would close the door on another chapter of our lives and it went by ever so fast. Before we knew it the International Removal Company had been and gone, our suitcases all packed up and ready to leave. The South Island was beckoning, we said goodbye to the house and to Tammy as the new owner was more than happy to keep her so a happy ending all round. We all piled into Sue the Subaru with a tinge of sadness and made our way down to Wellington where we would catch the ferry across to the South Island. No motor home that time around just a couple of tents and our worldly belongings to get us through the next two weeks.

The South Island

Well we are slowly coming to the end of the Bairds New Zealand adventure; I hope that you will finish to the end with us. In fact we are now at the final instalment of our New Zealand journey so I shall now take you on a tour of the South Island. I hope that these holiday add inns are not too boring but I am after all writing about all of our experiences during the past couple of years and anyway on the plus side you may get some good travel routes to inspire your adventures.

The South Island holiday was a must for us just like Australia; it would have been crazy not to go while we were so close. The biggest hindrance we had on our minds when starting our tour from Picton was the fact we had not at that point received our passports back from the Canadian High Commission, we had two weeks left in New Zealand and time was certainly of an essence. We could not fly anywhere without them and we had no house to go back to and no job for that matter so as you can imagine we did have a big weight on our shoulders.

Our next door neighbours or should I say ex next door neighbours were the religious type and trustworthy so our return address for our passports was their address and we made it plainly clear that if the passports should arrive they were to phone us immediately. With all of our instructions given and with time running away from us we could only try our best to have a happy holiday.

The ferry over to Picton was pretty plain sailing, no seasickness on anyone's part as the sea was as calm as it could be, and at times almost motionless. We had been well versed prior to the trip that the part of sea between the two islands was at its worst the worst stretch of sea in the world so we were slightly apprehensive about the three-hour crossing. We were pleasantly surprised and made it outside onto the deck to catch our first glimpse of the South Island. The journey across that stretch of open water is relatively short as the main time taker is navigating through the Queen Charlotte Sound. The scenery was amazing and so were the many private and I am sure exclusive properties that lined the banks in their very own private Idaho.

After an easy sail we arrived at Picton mid morning and after a quick drive through the town we set about getting down to Kaikoura for our first nights camping. On the way we stopped at Blenheim to buy some lunch, pies of course as you know by now we have to sample the pies in most places we visit and Blenheim was no exception!

Before out holiday started we purchased two books on New Zealand and they had the must see sights along the way. Just outside of Blenheim in Riverlands there stands a Cob Cottage. It is a real picture and furnished completely in late 1800's style, it is a very small little cottage but gives you a great feel of what life must have been like back then. I am sure in those days though the occupant would not have heard the busy traffic on the main road just outside their front door! The cottage was built for a local farmer in 1860 and would have been made out of a mixture of puddle clay and straw that was made into bricks or packed between forms.

Photographs done with we turned Sue the Subaru back onto the main highway south down to the famous lobster place near Kaikoura, the famous lobster place that a famous Scottish comedian visited on his three wheeled motorbike tour of New Zealand a couple of years back. It was well worth the visit, we sat looking at the ocean whilst munching on freshly caught crayfish cooked in garlic butter, and I can still taste them now! To clarify in New Zealand they call lobsters crayfish, in the UK we know crayfish as those smaller versions of lobsters that inhabit the canals eating all the native fish eggs

The Kaikoura coast is far from the calm seas we left back in Gisborne, the surf is littered with rocks and the sea rough. However despite the testing condition's Kaikoura's peninsula is home to one of the most assessable seal colonies in New Zealand and well worth the short drive. The seals look so harmless as they lie sunbathing but they could and would cause you serious harm if you over stepped over the distance mark.

Crayfish snack finished we found the only campsite in Kaikoura that had a vacant tent spot, it was busy, very busy and the tent area was like a tin of sardines. It was not so good, privacy was non-existent and as we are a very private family we found the whole squashed tent syndrome a bit hard to tolerate. Nevertheless we had no choice but a second night in Kaikoura as planned would not be. Things got even more claustrophobic when it came time to prepare our evening meal, as the shared kitchen area for the campers was rather large but heaving and each cooker was in use. There was nothing else for it but to stand amongst the other not too patient cooks and wait for that spare cooking ring. I am so glad I was not cooking a three-course al la cart menu! Eventually I was able to take over a ring and hastily cooked our mince and pasta sauce that we enjoyed in the privacy of our zipped up tent with the entrance facing a bush! After the usual washing dishes in the still busy kitchen we settled into bed for the night hoping that the morning would come around quickly so we could pack up and leave. With the first rays of sun glinting through the clouds the next morning that is exactly what we did.

From Kaikoura we sped along at a good rate, only stopping to take in the ocean views along the way and to stop at the large brick church of St Paul's in the small town of Waipara. The small church was built between 1812 and 1905 and had not lost any of its character. In 1939 archaeologists at Waipara discovered five complete Moa skeletons, so for such a small place it had a huge history to boast.

We were by that time not too far from Christchurch and due to the amount of places to visit there we did plan to stay for a couple of days. Time enough to see all that there is to see in the English heritage style city. The only problem we encountered upon arrival was the lack of camp spaces, Christchurch had many campsites but the majority of them were completely booked up. What we did not know or rather what we had not realised was it was a long weekend and as New Zealanders do they go away on long weekends! After numerous phone calls we booked a tent pitch with a campsite just outside of the city. We were slightly apprehensive about the campsite as it had quite a few places left and on occasions there can be a very good reason for that. However upon arrival we were more than pleasantly surprised, it was a lovely campsite, with new English owners and in true British style they had made a real good go of their new business and it showed. The advantage at that particular camp was we could choose from numerous tent pitches and we chose a nice area, next to the second kitchen and laundry/toilet block.

There were two ablution blocks on the site and our choice was to be near the smaller and less busy one.

It was a lovely sunny day and after the tents were put up, beds blown up and the general getting sorted out done we took a walk around the campsite. We let the children have a play on the playground and then headed off into the city. Our food stock was diminishing and we needed milk and bread so a stop at the supermarket was in order. It was by then late afternoon so once we had slowly wandered around the supermarket browsing it was time to go back to base to cook dinner of venison stew.

Whilst we had been out a new family had arrived at the campsite, they were not camping in tents but rather staying in one of the chalets just to the side of our tenting area. The chalets were not too close so the residents from them did not invade on our privacy too much. It just meant that the new family would be sharing the kitchen area with us and that was fine, at first!

It did not take us too long to figure out that the new arrivals were slightly odd, in fact slightly odd is probably an understatement! They looked like gypsy cross stuck in a major time warp type individuals wearing extremely worn old fashion clothes and shoes that had gone well past their best. Their car was no different; a very old banger indeed so from then on that poor family became the butt of our jokes. They lacked manners also that does not help social skills or bring the best out of people. So the weird family from who knows what millennium had arrived.

I had the joy of cooking dinner alongside the families mum and to break the ice I politely as you do said "Hello" to her and she totally ignored me! That was fine by me, as I felt uncomfortable with her presence. In this day and age dressing and behaving like that only draws attention to the fact that you somehow do not or do not want to fit into present day society unless you are of a certain religion but they were not, they were just strange. I have nothing against the true gypsy's of this world, they do not lack respect for others in the way that family did and they live a very exiting life visiting many different places.

I had timed our meal well, I was serving up at the same time as they had finished up and so they left us in piece to eat and talk about them! We must sound like a right bunch of gossips but everybody in life talks about those who are stranger than normal and those who say they don't are just liar's.

Meal finished, dishes washed dried and put away we tucked the children up into they're sleeping bags and sat outside with a bottle of wine whilst being well wrapped up in a blanket. The weather had turned chilly by evening and we had noticed the temperature dropping the further South we travelled. After a good few glasses of the red stuff Jack Frost had found his way in through the blanket fibres and it was time to get tucked up into bed. The only time we really felt the cold was when we were getting un-dressed, toilet visits in the night and of course getting dressed again in the morning. We had adopted a new way of getting dressed in the morning called get your clothes on in bed and it did work. There was no bare flesh exposed to the elements so none of us really got too chilly, thankfully.

I do not know if it is a British trait but Lance and I cannot function in the mornings until we have had a cup of tea or two, my father Arthur drinks about three cups in the morning! A hot cup of steaming tea helps the system prepare for the daily schedule ahead and after a few cups of tea, a cup of coffee and breakfast we set off to explore the city of Christchurch for the day.

Navigating the city outskirts was not too challenging. You will know by now that I always dread having to be the map-reader but I dread even more the prospect of driving in a huge city that I do not know so map reading it was and I managed to direct us to a parking zone that was not too busy and not a great walk to the Cathedral Square, so perfect all round.

Christchurch immediately appeared English, the architecture of the buildings is just amazing and with the Avon River running through made it a very romantic city.

What we did not know at that point is that the weirdo family had also decided to go to the city that day and we could not believe our eyes when we saw them in front of us. We actually saw them on several occasions throughout that day which was really strange. Were they the stalkers or were we the stalkers? Their bright red hair and their bright red car was unmistakable and they could be spotted a mile away so after a while we tried to avoid being in the same place but it was not that successful.

We hoped that a ride on the tram would foil their stalking activity so we waited at the bus stop or I should say tram stop for the next available tram. The trams in Christchurch had carried passengers since the line was built in 1905 and in recent years the tramline was reconstructed on a 2.5-mile loop that takes visitors past the best tourist areas and the short ride did not disappoint. Along the way you get a running commentary from the tram driver giving the history of the buildings and gardens that you pass by so as well as being a good rest for the legs it provides you with a small amount of Christchurch's history. We did very well that day or rather the children did. They have smaller legs than us adults so walking can become tiring for them but they enjoyed the sights and sounds of Christchurch just as much as we did. The clincher for them was the tram ride and the botanical gardens where they could let off some steam in the playground and just generally run as free as we would allow.

One place we will most definitely make an effort to visit again would be Christchurch. I think its unique English feel, and the wonderful rich culture is very homely and appealing and we have mentioned going back for the Rugby World Cup in 2011 if all goes to plan. We support the All Blacks rugby team more than any other rugby team and we only spent eighteen months in New Zealand so they must have impressed us somehow! It would be such an experience to watch them play on their own turf.

With map in hand we left Christchurch and headed inland to drive through the magnificent Raikaia Gorge that was on the way to our next map pin point Geraldine. It was easier for us to get onto the inland road from Christchurch, as we had not planned to visit Timaru. It was not because we did not want to visit Timaru but we did want to see where our old boxer dog Jake had moved to in the small village of Twizel and that meant driving further inland from Geraldine and by-passing some of the main road south. It was a small diversion but it was the right choice, the inland scenery was breathtaking and definitely not to be missed.

Geraldine was in itself a real gem; it was a proper tranquil rural town and a real surprise. The accommodation that we had arranged prior to arriving was not to be disappointing in the least, it was as described a modern detached two-bedroom bungalow and to us a home away from home. It was one of those places that I would recommend to anyone and for that reason I have included the contact details on the resource page at the back of this book.

Geraldine was a remarkable place; it boasted a cheese maker, chocolate maker and a recognised fruit product producer and of course there were the tasters! The children thought Christmas had come as they were allowed to taste jams, juices, cheese's and a whole array of other local produce and it goes without saying we enjoyed it also! The piece de resistance came in the local knitwear shop and I remember making quite a few notes in there. It is famous for having the world's largest jumper (in 2007 anyway) measuring from wrist to wrist sixteen feet and it was a feature in the 1999 Guinness Book of Records. That was not all to that little knitwear shop. The owner had recreated the Bayeux Tapestry using one million, five hundred thousand pieces of spring steel, it took twenty years to complete, weighs two hundred and thirty kilograms and measures in at thirty three point eight meters in length. If that was not enough of an achievement through years of researching history they have depicted the last eight meters of the Bayeux Tapestry. As according to historians the last sections of the original were never discovered, three months of missing history carefully depicted by a father and daughter team. We thoroughly enjoyed our only day and night at Geraldine but with other places to see we had to say goodbye. However it was a place we have put on that to see again list and we will make sure that we will see Geraldine again.

Our next stop was at Lake Tekapo; a slight disappointment as we thought the area was rather bleak but I suppose the horrible freezing rain and the howling winds did not help paint a good picture of the place. It did have a little church that you could walk in and out of and a monument in honour of the sheepdog as without those herding dogs no farmer could have any livestock on the land. We did not hang around too long as it was too cold and the rain very heavy so back into Sue we got and away we went.

You may remember further back in the book that we left Gisborne with a slight air of concern about our passports and the worry that we would not receive them in time to fly back home to the UK. You will also remember that we asked our neighbours to let us know immediately the minute that they arrived. Well we had spent by that time nearly a week worrying about those passports, thinking we would be cancelling our flights and everything so we decided to give our neighbours a call to see if they had arrived or not but as we had assumed that they would let us know we assumed that they had not arrived. So whilst driving past Lake Benmore Lance finally got through on the mobile phone and discovered that the passports had indeed arrived, the day after we left! So we had spent all those days fretting whilst our passports sat on the neighbour's shelf awaiting our pick up! On the other hand we could finally breath easy and enjoy the remainder of our trip in a relatively stress free state.

Talking of our old neighbours they had mentioned to us to drive up to Mount Cook. The road leads off to the left just before you reach Twizel and we did intend to go up and see the mountain. That day the weather was just not at its best so Mount Cook would not have been visible to us even if we had of driven up to view it. In one way it was a good thing, as the extra time needed to go up the Mount Cook road would have really left us in a very tight time situation so we abandoned that idea.

The road from Geraldine to Twizel was awfully long, it was a real struggle of a day as the quality of the roads were not great and not for the first time Laura was not coping with the twists and turns so well. It was one of those routes that apart from the mountains and lakes that are admittedly scenic there is little in the way of places to stop for a break. Combining that and the lack of campsites we had to really drive that day and after a rather impromptu fish near the local salmon farms we had a flying tour of Twizel before once again laying some rubber on the road.

I have forgot to mention our visit prior to Twizel to an out of the way salmon farm where we tried raw salmon, soy sauce and wasabi, not to everyone's taste but it was ok and we did finish our rather generous serving. The salmon was good quality as it lived in the channels that the ice melt water travelled along so the fish had to swim against rather strong currents and that kept them fit. The effort needed by the fish's muscles to stay in one place and not be swept away stopped the build up of large fat deposits in the flesh that spoils so many farmed salmon. To treat ourselves that evening we purchased a whole salmon to enjoy. We have never been able to afford a whole salmon as in the UK they are very expensive so we thought it would be a nice change from the usual fillets.

Anyway back to the route. Oamaru was our next real destination but trying to find a place to hang our shoes for the night proved rather impossible despite our efforts much earlier in the day so in the end the only place we could find that had a space was a motel located on the main road just outside of Oamaru. It was near enough for us to travel back to Oamaru that evening to have a look around and view the little blue penguins that the area is known for.

We actually arrived at Oamaru late; well I say late it was around 6pm and already the light was starting to fade. The motel was indeed just a short drive out of Oamaru and on the scale of one to ten on the clean/comfort scale the motel scored about a five so not bad but not too good either. The task of unpacking the car was a daily routine and a tiresome one at that after a few days of doing it but it was part and parcel of travelling around in a car. Lance organised the cases and bedrooms whilst I tended to the evening meal of fresh whole salmon, potatoes and peas. What I did not know was the oven in the motel room was not working to its full capacity and after thirty minutes of cooking time the salmon had barely cooked unlike the rest of the meal that was. I turned the oven up in hope that the fish would be cooked quicker but the oven was just not responding. We had never had a whole salmon before and my idea of serving a well-cooked and well cared for fish was not on the menu that night. We could not wait for hours for the fish to cook so in the end I had to scrape the flesh off the bones and microwave it, what an absolute travesty. The microwave cooking turned a once perfect whole salmon into a pile of over cooked chewy fish that you would have thrown back at a waiter if served it in a restaurant. Needless to say it was a disaster and not an enjoyable meal.

The evening was going fast and although we had well and truly missed the penguin talk and the flood lit area on the beach by the time we had eaten and cleaned up we thought we would still go to Oamaru beach to see if we could see those little penguins. We were in luck as some of the little fellows were still finding their place to sleep for the night among the rocks and shrubbery. We stayed for a good fifteen minutes watching them and taking some photos before we left them be and headed back to the motel for the night. The next morning I was glad to be leaving that motel. It was just not clean enough for me and I did not sleep too well as the room was cold due to the heater being set on a timer so as soon as it slightly warmed up it switched off, a money saving scheme for the management.

We were now almost at the bottom of the South Island and finding the scenery a stark contrast to that above Christchurch. More rugged and definitely much colder so the tent was left in its package and we opted to stay at motels rather than freeze in a tent from that point on, it was a wise idea.

Our next port of call was to be Moeraki. Those of you who have been to the South Island of New Zealand or familiar with some of the famous landmarks there would recognise Moeraki for its boulders that were formed over four million years ago. They are quite amazing perfectly spherical balls of limestone lying on the beach and in the surf. Timing to see the boulders in the sea is rather crucial and for once we arrived at that crucial time. If the tide is in then the boulders are hidden and unless you want to spend hours hanging around you will only be able to view the beached boulders. Moeraki as we had thought was busy with many people milling around, standing on the boulders to have their pictures taken and generally admiring such a natural spectacle.

I am going to digress for a moment here from the above paragraph just to warn you in case you think I have missed something! I am sure that most of you have had at some point seen someone somewhere or bought a new car and for some reason you see those people or person or the same type of car you have just bought everywhere! It is because you notice them easier as you have been exposed to that particular thing, for example we bought a Renault Laguna back in the UK and afterwards we noticed lots of Renault Laguna's about. Anyway I hope that makes sense but the reason behind that mumble is the weirdo family, they had the most unmistakable red car and to our utter disbelief that car was parked in the Moeraki Boulders car park and to make the situation even more weird they seemed to be everywhere we were. It was very odd indeed that we kept on seeing that family.

The shop was much the same as any other tourist shop, full of expensive bits and bobs so we just purchased a couple of postcards to keep as a souvenir and continued along Highway 1 to Dunedin with its famous "Worlds Steepest Street" known as Baldwin Street, would we walk it? Dunedin is the South Island's second city and is known well for its Edwardian and Victorian architecture and it is home to New Zealand's first University that teaches worldwide students. In fact just on first glance it is apparent that Dunedin is a major University City with many students from all walks of life.

As we found in Christchurch accommodation was hard to find in Dunedin as that particular weekend a big motor cross championship was being held so finding anywhere to stay was impossible. It had been a struggle on a few other occasions during the trip to find a bed but we always managed to find something but on that occasion luck was not on our side. Our plan to spend two days in Dunedin was not likely and we had to arrange accommodation far away in Balclutha for that evening. Anywhere within an easy drive of Dunedin was fully booked so another long day of driving was necessary in order to find a suitable motel to stay at. Despite the knowledge we had a major drive ahead we would not leave Dunedin without seeing the sights and of course attempting to walk up that famous steep street.

After looking at a couple of cathedrals and a few shops we felt energetic enough so we drove along the stretch of road to Baldwin Street. In all honesty all the streets along that road were

incredibly steep and for those who had to walk up them everyday I certainly did not envy them. We finally reached the street
and we were both in awe of it, Baldwin Street with its 1 in 2.86
gradient made the other streets appear very tame but we had
decided to walk it and walk it we did. The first part of the street
is actually not too bad but as the gradient increases those calf
muscles start to burn and I have to admit I felt very unfit and at
one point quitting really did cross my mind. The children
seemed to take it all in their stride and if Lance found it as hard
as I then he hid it well so I grinned and bared it finally making
it to the top on two feet and not on hands and knees. We have
the certificate on the wall to prove we did walk it! The sad tale
of the street is that some years a small proportion of the university students die whilst doing rather stupid things like going
down it in a shopping trolley. The students also hold an annual
Jaffa competition in which they race Jaffa's, little round chocolate orange balls. They roll them down the street and the first is
obviously the winner. I believe it is quite a spectacle when it is
in full swing.

On the way back from our most strenuous exercise to date
we had a little flurry of excitement when Lance turned onto a
one-way street to find all the traffic coming directly towards us!
A poor guy on his scooter must have had such a shock when he
saw us in front of him; so much so he nearly fell off he swerved
so badly. Thankfully and with not much time to spare before a
collision Lance managed to take the next street on the left that
took us back onto the main road out of Dunedin.

New Zealand's South Island was as beautiful as we had
thought; it was another world in comparison to the hustle and
bustle of the more populated North Island and less heavily populated by the Maori. Despite the beautiful places we had visited

so far there was not really anywhere that made us really regret leaving New Zealand for Canada. We felt so limited in Gisborne let alone very isolated and a move to the South Island would have been a mistake as we would have been further isolated and found the remoteness of some of the towns and villages too much. We knew very well that we could leave New Zealand in the knowledge that our choice of Canada was much better suited to us and we would never have that nagging feeling at the back of our minds asking "Should we have tried the South Island first?" By taking those two weeks to travel as much of the South Island as we possibly could we instilled a deep happiness that we had experienced such a unique diverse place. A place that was so far away from home and we felt on those grounds we could leave on a good note with no regrets.

We still had a week to go and Balclutha was our next stop after our Dunedin exertions, so I will now get us back on track. There is not too much really that I can write about Balclutha, it was a small town and we arrived on a Sunday so all the local shops were shut and to be perfectly frank the shops that we did see did not overly interest us too much. We were just happy to have caught the supermarket before it closed and to be able to relax in a very tidy two bedroom family unit at a very quiet motel. Quiet was the operative word as the place was empty; the reason being we assumed was the big event that was taking place in Dunedin. Peace and quiet is all we ask from a motel and we certainly got what we wanted. A nice clean tidy unit and that ever so important space that we enjoy so much.

Before I go any further along I would like to point out that certain areas of the South Island are very well known by extreme sport junkies, those individuals that get a thrill from throwing themselves off cliffs attached to a springy rope, you know the type. Well we were not too far away from those areas, mainly around the Queenstown location and above. There are also some great tramping experiences to be had in those mountains but with two young children we were limited to the amount of tramping we could tramp. Tramping basically means hiking to those who find tramping a rather silly word but that is what it is in New Zealand and we found it kind of funny, we would regularly as a means of amusement change the third letter to a U, yes I know very childish but it got us chuckling on many occasions when we were going for a short "tramp"!

By the time we had reached Gore the weather was awful, it has rained none stop and it was very bracing indeed once we were out of the car. However as those photographic opportunities arose we had to adhere by them and it was time to stand looking as happy as we could in the conditions next to the giant brown trout statue. The giant brown trout statue aptly placed not too far away from one of the best trout fishing rivers in the world. Anglers from all regions of the world visit Gore just to pit their wits against the cunning browns and to our amazement there was one lonely angler braving the weather to out wit an unwary fish. True dedication and nothing else I think applied in that case.

I must apologise for flitting from place to place since we left Christchurch but we were running a little behind our schedule and we had not been inspired enough to really spend much time anywhere else since that point. The weather was cold and although each place had its own little quirks a drive through or a quick stroll sufficed.

Gore was a turning point in the weather conditions and by the time we made it to Mossburn it had started to snow, a lot. We were nearing the impressive mountain ranges of the Fiordland National Park that lay out in front of us. That area we had been told was New Zealand's version of the Rocky Mountains of Canada so we were exited to compare notes on that statement. On a good note the area is an un-relentless picture of natures beauty, it is hard to describe the power and authority over the land that those snow peaked mountains impose as they stand like formidable giants watching over there domain. Manapouri was less impressive; our very expensive accommodation was just terrible due to a dirty unit with old-fashioned dated equipment that was as old as the geriatric owners. That run down ramshackle of a place for value for money was the most expensive place we stayed at during the whole holiday and the worst. We had initially planned on staying for two nights but one was enough, the boat trip to view the Milford Sound was expensive as was everything in the Manapouri area so after a restless night we headed to Queenstown. Surely we would not be disappointed there.

It was hard to cast too many bad points over Queenstown as it was a gorgeous place, nestled in the mountains and next to Lake Wakatipu with its multi million dollar homes lining the banks. You could not argue that Queenstown was not a very sort after location but it was an exclusive place and unless you had a high bank balance living there or indeed renting a home would be out of most peoples grasp. It was expensive in the shops as you would expect from a thriving tourist area but that did not stop us from sampling the local wears. The local wears being the old fashioned sweet shop that made the most delightful fudge. With very sweet teeth and more than likely high blood sugar we drove further along to Arrowtown.

Now earlier I mentioned that we had not visited anywhere on the South Island that would have changed our minds about leaving New Zealand and that did not change. However if we did feel inclined to live on the South Island and money was no object we would have chosen without a doubt Arrowtown over anywhere else. Arrowtown is one of Otago's most picturesque towns and is unfortunately over shadowed by the bigger better-known Queenstown if you ask me. The history is a remarkable tale of wealth due to the discovery in 1862 of one of the richest sources of alluvial gold in the world. In fact many of the local historical houses have been nicely converted into tourist shops. For such a small place what it lacks in size it more than makes up for in the history and the beauty of the place and I would say that a visit to the South Island is not complete until you go to Arrowtown. It is an absolute must.

The scenery in that area of the South Island with the lakes, the mountains and the forests are stunning but to compare them to the Canadian versions cannot be justified to me at all. New Zealand does not have mountains like the Rockies and Canada does not have mountains like New Zealand and those who say that they are alike are wrong. The mountain ranges of Canada and New Zealand are beautiful in their own way and to compare them on equal ground is a travesty to both. In my eyes there is no comparison between them only a raw individual unique beauty.

In true New Zealand fashion the roads did not stay travel friendly for long. Once we left Arrowtown they merged into the winding snakes that we dreaded on every trip and according to the map once we reached the West Coast they would take a further turn for the worst. So it was time at that point to make sure we had a steady supply of sick bags handy for those who could not cope with the never ending roller coaster ride that we had to endure over the next few days to follow.

Wanaka was a small place but again like many other places along that side of New Zealand very tourist orientated. In a way that over indulgence of all things touristy spoils the original nature of a place but on the other hand without the tourist's the South Island's economy would be very poor and those places I mention would not be overly appealing to the many tourists that flock to that region of New Zealand each year.

Just outside of Wanaka on the main Highway 6 we came across one of those adrenalin junkie spots, a bungee jump, that to me was terrifying to say the least but we pulled in and had a look to see what all the fuss was about. The bungee centre was good and you could actually go and view the jumpers as they jumped from the bridge into the canyon and river below. It was funny to watch but to me an unusual past time and not a natural thing to do at all. However all that did complete the jump appeared exhilarated and more often than not would have a second jump. I felt very uncomfortable standing at the edge of a shear drop only protected from certain death by a pane of glass that I am sure was reinforced to avoid any nasty accidents. We stood facing the bridge so we could see the jumpers clearly from the start of their jump to the time that they got picked up by a boat on the river below. It was not for me and after around twenty minutes of watching I could not stand anymore. Anxiety about the drop had set in and I was suffering from panic on a small scale so we left those to face their fears and I took mine back to the car to gather my self together.

The drive from Wanaka was pleasant enough for us all. We had not at that point hit any major snakes in the road and the surroundings were nice on the eye with the road being sided by Lake Wanaka to the left with the mountains of Mount Aspiring National park as a backdrop and to the right Lake Hawea.

All was well until we reached the Haast Pass and then as expected the roads turned nasty. It was not a pleasant experience and although the map indicated the distance to Haast Village was not too far it was a never-ending journey. The roads were narrow and the views were not great due to the dense forest surrounding us. The steep climbs and dramatic descents were not good at all for Sue the Subaru or for our contorting stomachs. We were behind a couple of motor homes and it was not long until we both mentioned that we could smell burning. We commented that the camper van in front of us must have had burning brakes so it was a relief when we finally got to the bottom of what seemed a slope from hell. The camper in front of us did have hot brakes but it was not their brakes we could smell. It was Sue's and that was apparent as soon as we stopped as there was thick black smoke billowing out from Sue's wheels and Lance even saw a few small flames, Sue's brakes were on fire! At first I did not quite comprehend what was happening or the possible severity of the situation. We were at the bottom of a very steep hill surrounded by thick forest with of course no mobile phone signal! The only relief was that we had pulled into a small car park with other tourists who had stopped to see the waterfall amongst the trees. If the worst happened and believe me I had it all going through my head that Sue and all our belongings should perish in a fireball, somebody would help. The only thing to do was to take off the wheel trims to allow more air to pass through and cool the brakes. It was our lucky day and it worked so after a rest of about fifteen minutes Lance felt it would be safe enough to continue along to Haast Village taking it slightly slower and using the gears to slow down rather than be heavy on the brakes. The road did not get much better from that point on but they did not get any worse and that was a huge relief as I am sure that Sue would have been in serious trouble if the roads had worsened.

After a gruelling drive on a never-ending road we pulled up outside a café at the village of Haast just in time for Laura to be very sick. Laura bounces back from travel sickness quickly once she has been sick and after only a few minutes she was happily eating toasted sandwiches in the café. There was nothing in Haast Village to see so after a bite to eat and a drink of hot coffee we reluctantly made our way back onto the highway.

That same day despite the gruelling road we made good headway and visited Fox Glacier before settling for the night at Franz Josef also home to another rather impressive glacier. In both locations you can take a helicopter ride that fly's over both the Fox and Franz Josef glaciers among others in the area. Those helicopter rides are very expensive; I am talking hundreds of dollars so we opted for the inexpensive pair of legs that we were equipped with to carry us to view the glaciers. We captured some wonderful images of both glaciers from ground level that were good enough for us. We did not have the privilege to view the glaciers from the air but I was happy with having the money in my purse rather than blowing it all on a ten minute helicopter dash. That night we slept very well after the previous days nightmare drive and dreamt that Arthur's Pass with the resident Kea's would prove a worthy trip. The decision to enter Arthur's pass from the West Coast side of the South Island was made early in our tour. The other route is from the Christchurch side and not as scenic or so we had been told. Either way there was little chance I could miss going there due to my father's name of Arthur and having a photograph taken next to the sign for him.

I am going to go straight to Arthur's Pass here. You may wonder why and I will explain as best as I can whilst keeping it simple. In all honesty the rest of the journey from Franz Josef to the turning for Arthur's Pass was nothing to write home about and really not worth including in this section. There was only one area that I remember well along that stretch and that was only due to the fact that we got a free meal of venison at Lake Ianthe. It was there that we came across some deer hunters butchering their kills and they kindly gave us a nice piece of red deer fillet for our tea. Other than that the road just blended into one, a mix of turns, forest, more turns and more forest. If you ever visit the West Coast you will understand what I mean about the route from Franz Josef to the turn off for Arthur's Pass, or you will disagree with my take on that particular stretch and that is acceptable as we all have different opinions. When we visit the South Island again we will probably not tour the West Coast a second time. For what you see in our opinion the effort of the journey along that road far outweighs the need to see the sights that are along it. Again each individual is different and we are all entitled to our own opinions, some may love that region but for us it was a battle of attrition.

Nearly Home and Dry

Our time on the South Island was by then coming to a close and indeed so was our time in New Zealand. We still had four days to go and with the worst of the roads over and done with on the West Coast we could relax once again and take in the sights and sounds that the area around Arthur's Pass had to offer us.

The trip to Arthur's Pass was at times a little hairy as the road became steep at one section and for every steep bit there is always the downside, literally! The downside was bad and we had visions of those burning brakes again but we worried need-lessly as our trusty transport Sue the Subaru managed the treacherous descents well. Arthur's Pass was again a little disap-pointing. The views from the top road before you make your decent into Arthur's Pass itself are worth getting the camera out for but we were slightly down beat at the place itself. The kea's were not in huge numbers as we had believed but we did see one crossing the road outside of the café and on our return we stopped at Death Corner. A great vantage point to get a good look at the Otira viaduct that makes travel through the Otira gorge to Arthur's Pass township easier than in the days of old. An interesting piece of information is the reason why that point on the road is called Death Corner. Apparently and please do not hold me to this a young girl was killed when thrown from the horse and carriage she was travelling in, it turned over on that very corner. A story whether true or not is good to tell and believable when you actually have travelled on that section of road yourself. The lookout is a really good spot to get the viaduct in its full glory and if you are lucky enough like we were a couple of keas may drop in to say hello. As we usual do in most places we did not heed the no feeding sign and fed the hungry birds crackers although I do not think the spicy pepper ones were to their taste.

The journey back from Arthur's Pass took sometime. It is a fairly good drive off the main road but the difference being the roads are easy enough and we once again made good time.

I was aware that the West Coast of New Zealand was well known for its seafood and I was going to make sure I would sample any seafood critters if I came across any on route. So my eyes stayed constantly peeled like a real hunter-gatherer type in anticipation of a shellfish meal. It was not too long before we could see that the rocks in the surf were covered in black blankets, literally nearly every rock was smothered. As we discovered the black blankets were huge colonies of mussels. I had found my seafood dinner for that night and we hastily collected enough for a meal before the tide came in washed us all away into the Tasman Sea never to be seen again.

From the mussel collecting beach we stopped a couple of kilometres up the road at the Pancake Rocks Blowholes tourist spot and as you can guess from the name the rocks have taken on the appearance of stacked pancakes. It is a rare sight and the walk provides a good amount of exercise for those car squashed legs. Driving long distances in one day does not do the circulation much good so a quick stroll or tramp should I say does do you the world of good.

Tramp over and with mussels in tow we arrived in Westport just after 5pm and with little time to waste out came the cooking equipment to cook our two-day-old fillet of venison and our freshly picked West Coast mussels. Do not be confused here as I was not cooking a new fangled concoction by putting them together but making a venison curry and garlic, white wine and cream mussels. During the mussel preparation time of de-bearding them one of the children noticed a small little crab that they took pity upon. The little crab was saved from the boiling liquor and it was carefully placed in a jar for its return back to the water after our meal. If anyone was watching us that evening they must have thought our behaviour rather strange to say the least. Lance with torch in hand led Josh to the waters edge to release the little crabby into the river miles away from its home among the mussels. The poor thing probably did not last long but it had a chance and the children felt happy that they had saved it from a fate worse than death. So after the successful release we drove back to the motel and settled down for the night, as the next day would also entail a rather long drive.

Bright and early the next morning we left Westport and the West Coast and continued along Highway 6 that skirted alongside the Buller River. The road was very narrow at times and went into a single lane on a couple of occasions due to a few very scary rock overhangs that made us a little uncomfortable. In time the road once again became easy to handle and before long we were nearing the quarter of the way mark just before Murchison.

We had no idea that there was a swing bridge along that road and we soon came across it. Lance is a stickler for all things daring despite the fact that he is actually very nervous about going on anything that is high but he had to go and see if he could walk across that swing bridge along with the children! I was not going to chance it and stayed well clear of the bridge in my usual passive manner or should I say panic manner. That particular swing bridge that crosses the Upper Buller River is the longest swing bridge in New Zealand and from start to finish it measures one hundred and ten metres long. I have to admit ten metres long is enough for me I am such a scaredy cat.

With the mission of the bridge cross complete in good time and after Lance had got his colour back we stopped in Murchison for a bite to eat and to read up in the café about the local history of which they certainly had. In 1929 Murchison was struck by a huge earthquake measuring 7.8 on The Richter Scale, it was devastating to the community and seventeen people lost their lives with many others injured. The surrounding landscape was altered beyond recognition and the scars from that earthquake can be clearly seen today. New Zealand is a hot spot for earthquakes and whilst we lived there we experienced a few shakes but nothing that worried us greatly. One has to remember though that in New Zealand the risk of a major earthquake was an everyday factor among the other natural phenomenon such as tsunami's and volcanic eruptions!

With only three more nights to go we needed to be relatively close to Picton and we found Richmond to be just right. Easy access to get onto the Golden Bay road and close enough to Picton for a short drive to the motel there for the last day and our final night on the South Island.

During the trip we had been on occasion more than lucky with our accommodation and the holiday park we had chosen in Richmond was no exception. It was a cheerful and bright detached three-bedroom bungalow that was actually not that far off in size to Waiteata Street so again it was a nice home away from home. Due to our late arrival into Richmond we had little time to explore further than the local mall and for Lance to purchase a new digital camera that was on offer, or that is what I got told anyway! One area that was a must to visit was Sandy Bay just passed Motueka on the north Highway 6. It was a place recommended by a friend of mine who said it was like a tropical island and from what we had seen on the Internet she was not going to be wrong.

With a nice picnic lunch prepared and a flask of coffee made we drove to Sandy Bay. It was another one of those shock and horror moments when you realise that a leisurely drive turns into a waking nightmare. We thought the roads on the West Coast were bad, they paled into insignificance compared to the road to Sandy Bay. Awful is not the word, twisty is not the word, loop the loop is more than fitting. The road literally went around the mountain; round and round and round we went until we finally came to a stop at yes a very beautiful tropical location. Rightly guessed Laura's first place was to be the toilet and she was very poorly indeed. Sandy Bay was as named a sandy bay with clear blue water and fine golden sand and very busy with lots of families taking advantage of the tranquil setting. And there were the Baird's feeling rather delicate eating their picnic on a bench surrounded by hungry wasps. No matter where you go in the world you can guarantee as soon as you sit down and open that picnic basket the local wasp population will be there to annoy the hell out of you. In between mouthfuls of sandwich we swatted at the wasps, calmed Elijah down who was hysterical due to the winged pests and nursed poor Laura who was a horrible shade of green. All in all the entire trip to Sandy Bay was a complete disaster. The trip back from Sandy Bay was no better as Laura vomited most of the journey and due to the sharp turns and heavy use of the brakes Sue the Subaru was once again protesting the rough handling and smoked away nicely. Understandably we did not attempt to travel any further and opted to return to the same holiday accommodation as the night before.

From Richmond continuing on Highway 6 there are two routes to get to Picton once you reach Havelock, have a look on a map and you will see what I mean. One route takes you straight across almost in a straight line, the other route is to stay on Highway 6 and do a sort of horseshoe shape down and then back up to Picton. In our opinion the latter route seemed very long-winded and after speaking to the holiday park manager we agreed to take the seemingly shorter more direct route across. Can you guess what is going to happen next?

It only seemed fair after such a terrible drive the day before to take the easier quicker route as we would arrive in Picton earlier that way and have more time to repack our suitcases ready for the journey back across to the North Island the following day. With regards to the panoramic views we could not have chosen a better route and after a few kilometres we stopped to have a fish in the most beautiful little harbour. We could not resist, as fellow fishermen would understand. It was a good spot and I hooked a nice size Kahawai to have for tea but the tide was on the way out and the best fishing time had passed so it was time to move on. All was well at that point and we were all in good spirits until the road started the loop the loop routine again and again Laura was in a state.

The lesson we learnt was not to look at a New Zealand road map and think that a road must be better because the map shows it is nice and straight. On the contrary if the road on a

New Zealand map does appear relatively straight to the naked eye don't bet any money that it is!

The last week of travel on the South Island had been hard on us especially Laura and it was a relief to not worry about unknown roads once back on the North Island. I cannot say the route from Napier to Gisborne is a breeze it is not as the roads are bad but we travelled that route regularly enough and we knew when to stop, so after the first few times no one suffered from travel sickness.

The ferry journey back was not as calm as the journey was to the South Island but once you have had a drink, something to eat and walked around the deck a few times the journey seems short and the ferry soon turns into Wellington.

We had two more nights in Gisborne left before we took a short flight from Gisborne to Auckland for our flight back to the UK for our months visit. For those last nights in Gisborne we stayed at a friends, the lady from the UK that I have mentioned earlier in the book. Their hospitality was well needed both in the comfort sense and for the company at a time when friendly support is needed. Although we were happy to leave Gisborne and New Zealand we had for the last eighteen months made it our home as best as we could. It was hard to say goodbye to those we called friends and to be truthful it was hard to say goodbye to New Zealand. Those feelings are natural and nothing to be ashamed about.

Our flight into Auckland was an early one and after getting the shuttle from the airport to the hotel that would be home for the next two nights we finally had the chance to gather our thoughts and get into the right frame of mind for the journey. A very long journey I must add back to family and friends in the UK. We were so tired that first night that we called for a take away meal, ate and went straight to bed falling asleep as soon as our heads hit the pillow.

The last and final day in New Zealand was spent in central Auckland seeing the Sky Tower and yes we did all go up to the highest level that is two hundred and twenty metres high. However I could not stand on the glass panels in the floor looking down at the city below as that was just asking too much. I had done well enough to get up there in the first place and that was something to be very proud of in my case. Auckland has the most amazing shopping malls but that is to be expected of such a huge city. The variety of cultures in Auckland was vast, the amount of people on the streets in Auckland was quite overwhelming and we found it rather daunting coming from such a small city in comparison. It was worth the feeling of being uncomfortable and cramped for a few hours as we did see a good proportion of Auckland's hot tourist spots. The time in Auckland went by so quickly and before we knew it we were at the airport waiting for our long haul flight. We knew what to expect so as expected we felt rather nervous and we did not look forward at so much time having to be spent in the air.

After what seemed like an eternity we finally touched down at Manchester Airport, UK at the beginning of May 2007. A welcoming crowd of smiling and crying family member's greeted us with open arms. I am not going to write about our month spent in the UK as to an outside reader it would not be of benefit to the story or be of interest I am sure. I can say though it was a fantastic time with plenty of good food and drink but most of all we must not forget the great company we had missed so much in the eighteen months we had been on the other side of the world. A whole month to catch up on family life before our next adventure began. Our time in the UK was over far too quickly and before long it was time to once again say goodbye.

Canada, Here we come

On the 1st of June 2007, we boarded our flight to Calgary, Canada and it was again a mixture of emotions. It was great to be finally on the last leg of our emigration journey but it was also extremely hard saying goodbye to our loved ones again. We had just spent a wonderful month with them and the feeling of belonging had slowly started to creep back. After being so far away in New Zealand it was a real joy to be back among all that was familiar to us.

Our flight to Calgary took eight hours and to be completely frank it was the worst flight we have ever been on and we have been on a few! It was not due to inclement weather or rowdy passengers but the airline itself. Unfortunately I cannot mention the particular offending airline as I don't want to be faced with a lawsuit but the service was utterly atrocious. We were provided with little drinks throughout the flight and most of us know apart from the airline in question that it is imperative that one drinks plenty of fluid on a long haul flight. Water was given out as if it was pure liquid gold and if you preferred any other drink other than tea and coffee you had to pay for it and it was not cheap! The so-called top of the range TV screens kept on crashing and as for the movie selection they were on a loop that just replayed every two hours. The best of it was if you actually wanted to hear your movie you had to buy the earphones, which I must add you could keep in case you ever felt the desire to travel with them again, not likely. Having a good old complain about our flight was our way I suppose of relieving some of the tension we were both feeling at that time. I have to add here that the three children had behaved well throughout the whole journey. I would not have blamed them in the slightest if they had behaved out of character as we were all completely fed up on that flight and very bored!

We had finally arrived at our destination and were preparing to go through customs. That was it, the big moment of truth. Were the Baird's going to finally be granted permanent residence in Canada? All our hard work over the past few years rested on that very moment in time and although all our documents were in perfect order we could not quite get rid of that feeling of uncertainty. That nagging thought that the officer stood in front of us could simply shatter our dream in a matter of minutes. Patiently we waited in line along with all the other arrival's ready to be called to the next available cubicle. The first Immigration officer we met was very nice and pleasant and he only looked at our passports and then us and stamped them just to say we had arrived in Canada. We were then guided through a set of doors and again had to queue behind the line, the part that we had been dreading our Immigration interview. There was a great deal of concern about our luggage by then, as you know you generally collect your belongings shortly after you have passed through the normal immigration section. Time was going by and we had visions of our luggage being taken off the luggage carousel and disappearing somewhere as the negligent owners had not been to collect it. After what seemed like hours we were eventually called over and quickly preceded to produce our documents to the gentleman officer behind the desk, who was also very chatty and jovial. The actual interview was to be fair not that bad, not as we had imagined it to be which was to be interrogated beyond belief. I suppose it was not really an interview as such either more a matter of answering some basic questions, our intentions in Canada, where were we going to live and have we visited before. The officer had to thoroughly check our ID and paperwork to establish that we were the same people as on the forms. That is a process you get very used to when you travel a lot.

The whole process took about fifteen minutes and despite what we thought you do not get your permanent residence card there at that time. They come in the post within four to six weeks but you do get the back copy of your immigration form stapled into your passport. Just in case there is some confusion here regarding what we got put in our passports back in New Zealand just before we left I will explain. Our passports had an Immigrant Visa inserted into them, the actual permanent residence is not finalised until you have completed the Immigration interview upon arrival in Canada.

By now we were all feeling tired, very thirsty and hungry especially the children who had by now begun to grumble, who could have blamed them? I was still feeling rough due to the good dose of antibiotics I had been taking for the pleurisy I had developed a week before we were due to fly. The double dose of antibiotics that were non negotiable if I wanted to make the flight in time, so it was a case of grin and bear the side effects of the sledge hammers banging in my head.

After a mad dash to collect our luggage, that had been neatly stacked on trolleys for us we headed for the airport hotel to recover from our eight hour ordeal in mid air and to de-stress after our immigration interview We arrived at the hotel to find that they had no record of our booking. We had stayed at that very same hotel when we went to Canada on our holiday in June 2005 and followed the same procedure in booking a room that second time as we had done the first time around. Contacting the hotel directly by e-mail and using the online booking service to secure a room. On neither occasion did they require payment details so we just assumed that the room would have been booked just as a room was booked back in 2005! Never assume anything. We booked another supposedly better room that was not that stunning for quite a bit more money, ordered an in room meal which was very much under par so it really was a fitting end to the day for us.

We woke up on the morning of the 2nd June feeling more refreshed and alert, ready for the final flight that would take us to Regina, Saskatchewan. The flight itself was only a matter of an hour and a half, which was fine, much better than the eight-hour flight the previous day. After arriving at Regina Airport and after collecting our luggage we sorted the hire car out that we had pre-booked and met up with the realtor who we had been in touch with for some months. She had arranged a rural rental property for us just outside of Regina within a fifteen-minute commute from the city and that was our next stop. On first appearances the property was lovely, big with plenty of area around the house, five acres to be exact and the interior was spacious and reasonably decorated. The biggest bonus was the fact that it was a rural property, in the countryside, exactly what we wanted. At that point our story becomes familiar with those programmes that we all have a chuckle about, you know the ones, a family move into their dream home to find it is riddled with all sorts of problems, a nightmare house.

It was not long before we realised that we had indeed been put into a property that had many problems. I am not saying that the realtor knew about the problems initially but she should have had the house inspected prior to us moving in. The biggest shock was the water, it was awful, and it stank of rotten eggs mixed with metal and was a lovely shade of tea. There was no way in the world that we were going to drink it. More distressingly for us was the fact we would not be able to wash in it or be able to wash our clothes. We had not come to Canada to live like tramps although I am sure that even they have access to clean water if they need it. So rather than relaxing in our nice rental property we spent the first week like coiled springs, ready to go off at the slightest thing. Our patience that was already wearing thin was about to be tested to the full by the tough Canadian bureaucracy of actually getting the simplest of things done. We arrived in Regina on a Saturday so there was little we could do until all the utility companies and banks were open on the Monday. So the weekend was spent sorting through our suitcases and generally trying to relax.

On the Monday morning we contacted the Saskatchewan telephone provider to establish a phone number as we had a great deal to sort out in that first week. That is when things got rather frustrating. We were informed that without any form of Canadian identification we could not be given a phone account. The main pieces of ID that they would accept were a Social Insurance Number (SIN) or a Health Card number, of which we had neither! The next step was then to contact the bank of our choice, as we wanted to open an account as soon as we could in order to transfer our funds. You may be able to guess here that yet again we were told that without any Canadian ID we could not open an account. In fact without having any

Canadian ID we could do absolutely nothing. It is crazy but we had passports, birth certificates and our permanent residence status confirmed in our passports as identification, however they were just not good enough.

There was nothing else for it. Our next move had to be to gain the ID required, so off we went into the city with a street map and no idea of where anything was and it was a nightmare. Neither Lance nor I are big city people and we both need a while to find our feet in such places. We did not have days to acclimatise to the city of Regina but a mere one day to sort the ID crisis out so you can imagine the air in the car was at times rather blue. We eventually managed to locate a car parking space after driving around the one-way system three times, which was no fun. We had luckily sourced the addresses of the places we needed from the yellow pages prior to setting off so that was one good thing. I am hopeless with directions and reading a map much to Lance's despair, something that I cannot deny and I don't try to.

First stop, the Health Card Centre as that piece of ID seemed to be at the top of the list. It was quite easy really just a form to fill out that required the usual basic information, names, ages and address of all of the family members and a signature. We did have to show our permanent residence status and provide our birth certificates so the lady could photocopy them for their records. Nothing taxing at all but it turned out that the medical cards were posted to you and that could take anywhere between four and six weeks, Great! Things were not getting any better. We then proceeded to the Government of Canada office were we were hoping to get our Social Insurance Number. We met with a very friendly lady who was sympathetic to our plight and helped us enormously. She interviewed Lance and I separately in order to establish whom we were and the children's details were provided by both of us. It was a simple twenty-minute process and although we were not given a card at that point we did get a sheet with our new SIN number on it, our SIN cards would take a week at the most to arrive.

The day did get better as we were able to set up a phone account and arrange an appointment with the bank. They would accept the SIN number as ID along with our British passports purely because we explained that we had applied for a Health Card but it would take a few weeks to arrive in the post.

I would like to explain here about the registration process for internationally trained Medical Laboratory Scientists here in Canada as it is a rather confusing matter and the next part of the book will not make much sense to you if I don't. Lance has to be registered with the Canadian Society for Medical Laboratory Science (CSMLS). They govern the occupation throughout the whole of Canada, now as well as being registered with the CSMLS he must hold a registration certificate with the provincial governing body. In the province of Saskatchewan that is the Saskatchewan Society for Medical Laboratory Technologists (SSMLT).

The CSMLS look at the education and employment history of the internationally trained scientist and evaluate him or her on the information provided to see if that person is the equivalent to the Canadian trained scientists. That information must be provided by the employer and the educational institute of the person to be evaluated and sent directly to the CSMLS. Getting that information to the CSMLS via the correct passage took us about ten months in all. A process that we started well in advance, as we knew that it would take some time. Once all of that information is received and evaluated a report is sent advising that you are either seen to be the equivalent of a Canadian scientist or informing you that you require more training to bring you up to the right level. Unfortunately Lance was required to undertake some refresher courses that he completed by June 2007 and successfully passed all six of them. He was then to be awarded a temporary certificate so he could register with the SSMLT. A temporary certificate is awarded because within twelve months of landing in Canada a five-hour exam has to be successfully challenged in order to become a full member of the CSMLS, they do not make it easy! Until Lance successfully passed that exam he could only be granted a temporary practising certificate with the SSMLT also.

Things started to look up and we felt like things were moving along, slowly but moving. We then had another blow. That time the blow came from Lance's new employer who kindly informed him with just over a week to go before he commenced work that there was more to him registering with the SSMLT than we had been initially told. In fact it was just such an unbelievable hitch. Lance could not start his new job until he applied for provincial registration, which we knew. Unfortunately we had been led to believe that that process was relatively quick and easy so we had not really hurried to start the process off. How wrong could we be? Lance needed to provide details of his education in university and his career record as a Medical Laboratory Scientist, details that we did not have as they were somewhere between New Zealand and Canada! Details we did not think we would need again so soon.

Someone somewhere was on our side as we remembered that we had brought with us all of Lance's documentation regarding his degree course and letters from his employers in the UK and in New Zealand. Thankfully we could in fact provide the majority of the information needed so he could become temporarily registered and start work. In order to speed things up Lance took the documents to the SSMLT office in Regina in person but we did not realise that they also required details from the CSMLS stating Lance's current registration status with them. Things were going to take a little while longer and he was due to start at the beginning of the following week, five days away! As things in Canada seem to take a long time to achieve it was a waiting game that left us feeling very frustrated.

The CSMLS were made aware that in order for Lance to be registered with the SSMLT and to be able to start work they had to provide his registration status. At that point you would think that the urgency of the situation would indeed spur on a swift response, not likely! It was again another fine example of Canadian bureaucracy on the slow.

On the other side of the coin was a happier face, it was another day we had been in Canada and we still felt the urge to stay. Frustrated yes, tired yes, unhappy in what we had done, not a chance! It may appear reading between the lines that it all sounds gloomy and depressing. There is always that first rocky start to any country, it is how it is, it is a test of strong will and yes it can be depressing. All bad points have good points, our good points to Canada is the next door neighbour telling us she saw a Moose in her garden, the howl of Coyote's in the night, the majestic Rockies a three hour flight away. It all becomes much clearer and brighter when you think about the good points.

Friendly Showers!

We had been in Canada for two weeks by that time and our water problem had not yet been fixed. We were forced to buy bottled water to use for drinking, cooking and to wash with as a shower or a bath was just not possible under the circumstances of rancid water.

The first week we went to a Mineral Spa in Moose Jaw. One to have a well-earned treat but more importantly for us all to have a good shower. We got into our swimmers and we were just about to enter the pool when the lifeguard ordered everyone out of the water. Such good timing as usual on our behalf as there was a storm overhead and due to the indoor pool being connected to the outside pool there was a small risk of getting fried if the lightening struck the water, yeah right! The children were disappointed but we all enjoyed the shower and the feeling of being clean once again! The question was, How long would the cleanliness last? How long is a piece of string?

Our nearest neighbour finally came across introducing herself and to let us know that if we needed any help of any kind then we should not hesitate to ask, you know the usual friendly neighbour spiel. She brought along her two dogs to say hello and despite their determined efforts to gain access to our house of horrors their efforts were fruitless! We chatted casually about Regina, the dreaded winter's that we had heard so much about before discussing our reasons for choosing Regina and Canada as a country. During the whole time my mind was not focused at all on what she was saying so I must have appeared very ignorant indeed. I was more concerned with the water and after about ten minutes I could not hold it in any longer. I told our poor welcoming neighbour what state our water was in, a cry for help I suppose and a hope that she may have been able to help. Help she did and we were extremely grateful for her offer of help. She had offered that if we needed anything then we should just ask but I am sure she did not think that we would be taking her up on that so soon. So when she offered us her shower for the morning we could not refuse. Some Canadian folk are very understanding and friendly, as I would certainly not let total strangers into my house let alone offer them a shower. It just shows how different cultures vary doesn't it?

Back home we continued to harass the realtor regarding the water problem. It was just getting ridiculous, the basic of amenities taken away for so long. As our rental property was rural the water supply came from a well in the back garden. The water was supposed to be taken through a softening system located in the basement, that system took out the impurities and some of the iron that is in the water in the Regina region. We finally had a visit from a company who informed us that the water softener was not working and it had not been working for sometime. That explained why things were so bad. The toilets had taken on a horrible yellow colour and the smell was just awful. The whole system had to be replaced and it was done a few days later, hooray! No more metallic eggy water for us.

It is important that before a move into a rental property the accommodation should be fully inspected, it is during those inspections that problems like ours would have been noted and rectified. We just assumed that the property would be fine but we now know better than to take it for granted.

We learned off our kind neighbour that well water can harbour some nasty bacteria and a sample of water should tested to check that it is within the safe drinking water guidelines. It really hit us then that there was a lot to be learnt about rural living in Canada. So much so that your water could be potentially very bad and make you all very ill.

We therefore took a sample to the local water-testing laboratory in Regina for analysis and although we did have to pay for the tests it put our minds to rest when the results came back that the water was safe to drink. We did continue to buy bottled water to drink nonetheless.

The water quality had improved greatly but we still did not want to drink it. Many rural households do in fact buy in water to drink, as the water in Regina is generally not that nice tasting. Once or twice a year water wells must be "shocked" with a chlorine solution in order to minimise the risk of dangerous bacteria such as E-coli growing that is obviously very bad for humans. The "shocking" process also prevents iron bacteria such as Crenothrix that eats through pipes developing. There are many other types of bacteria that can grow in a well so it is important that the "shock chlorination" process is followed annually. There were just some things that we could not have possibly researched or known to have researched before arriving in Canada. That was one example and I was a hundred percent sure that it would not be the last piece of information that we lacked.

The weeks had sure flown by and it was time to purchase our own vehicle and what a palaver that was to be! We had initially planned to buy another 4x4 just like the one we had in New

Zealand but we soon realised that they were too expensive so we would just have to settle for an ordinary car. Regina is a large place and I am sure that we must have gone to every garage over the space of a week. Time was running out, as the hire car return deadline was only a few days away at that time. In the end we settled on a Ford Taurus, a little more than we wanted to pay for an ordinary two wheel drive but we had little choice and I was fed up of trudging from garage to garage.

We returned the hire car back to the airport and settled the bill, well tried to settle the bill! The hire car company, a well-known company with branches all over the world did not accept cheque or debit card. Considering that was all we had we were put into a very awkward position as the bill was over a thousand dollars and we did not have that amount of money in raw cash. They tried in vain to convince us that there was enough money in our UK bank account to pay the bill and the lady even phoned her manager. Obviously we knew that there was not and like I said earlier our debit visa was only used to secure the booking in the first place, as we had planned to pay by cheque on return of the hire car. So there we were stood in Regina Airport rather annoyed that the company had no notice on the desk or for that matter informed us at anytime verbally or written into the agreement that they only accepted limited payment methods. As with most of these things the company to fault was trying to blame us for having insufficient funds to pay, what a cheek! After a long discussion with the manager it was arranged that we would draw out our daily limit from the hole in the wall and give them that. The remaining balance would have to be settled the next day. As we learned it is always advisable to ask the hire company what method of payment they accept. It is not the customer's responsibility to have to check such an important matter, as it should be clear in the company's small print. Double-checking does save red faces later on, something that we will bear in mind for the future.

Our new car was about to be tested by the rain. The road to our rural property was supposedly impassable when wet and there was a yellow sign stating that fact. It became clear that the car we had bought was totally unsuitable for the type of terrain we would be driving it on. The tires simply became balled up with the gluey mud and skidded all over the road as if it were on an ice rink. A slightly worrying issue considering the roads even in the wet are very good compared to what they are like in winter! Totally impassable if you do not have a 4x4 and we had just spent fourteen thousand dollars on a completely useless vehicle that would be hopeless in winter. Along with that notion the discovery that the back seats did not fold down to make the boot any use was a double blow. Like all newly bought vehicles new or used as soon as you drive them off the garage forecourt they lose thousands instantly, so trying to exchange our useless car for a 4x4 was not an option. We had to face the fact that we had made a mistake in buying the Taurus but with the pressure of time running out we had to buy something and yes we had bought in haste but what else could we have done? The car became a bit of a bug bare for us as it proceeded to have a few problems and we spent a lot of time back and forth to the garage were we purchased the car to have it repaired. The only problem was the garage was rather incompetent and did not bother to fix the problems properly. We really wished that we had not bought that car!

Lance had by then started work at the General Hospital in Regina and within the first week he had made his mind up that he did not like it there. He had spent his first day being trained about how the computer system works, all in one day so you can imagine after a few hours his brain was overloaded and information he was told hours earlier had been forgotten. Parking for him at the hospital appeared at first to be totally ridiculous as staff were given a parking pass so that they did not have to pay six dollars a day to work! Lance was told that his pass might take up to four weeks and with the six dollars a day fee in mind he went to security and after a discussion with them he got a parking pass. The biggest issue he had was within that first week he was taken to the wards and almost forced to take blood samples from babies some of which were premature. Lance has never undertaken any training in Phlebotomy and that was just an absurd and awful situation to put a new employee into. Lance was extremely stressed and upset and despite his obvious distress that he was more than uncomfortable with the issue his concerns were abruptly dismissed. He was told that there was no job for him if he was unable to carry out the Phlebotomy side of the position. A part of the job that he was never told about before applying or after being offered the post. The fact was Lance only wanted appropriate training so he could be confident and competent in such a delicate matter. Canadian Medical Laboratory Technologists undergo Phlebotomy training as part of their degree/diploma course so it was hard to understand why they were being so harsh with Lance for asking for structured training.

With all the problems with the car, Lance's new job and the house we were fast coming to the conclusion that Regina was not for us. We had missed the boat again regarding an acreage as prices in Regina had sky rocketed in the six months prior to our move. It sounds very familiar doesn't it, a slight déjà vu of Gisborne going on! Properties that would have sold for say two hundred and fifty thousand dollars were selling for three times that amount. Just ridiculous so we started to look for other jobs within Saskatchewan and within the other provinces.

It was not too long after searching the Internet employment engines that we found two jobs suitable for Lance to apply for. Both positions were in Manitoba, one was a Medical Laboratory position in Portage la Prairie and the other a Technologist position with a pharmaceutical company in Steinbach. After looking at both of these places on the Internet Lance sent off his application and resume and applied for both positions.

Properties in both locations were very much in our price range even the acreages so we did not need much persuasion to apply and we crossed fingers hoping! I suppose the other factor was that both Portage la Prairie and Steinbach are small cities whereas Regina is huge with a population at the time of writing around one hundred and eighty thousand people. Regina was just too big as both Lance and I have always been used too much smaller places such as Denbigh, North Wales that was our original home prior to leaving the UK. Even Gisborne in New Zealand was small in comparison. The city of Regina was just too intimidating and not our cup of tea at all. So all we could do was sit tight and wait until we heard any news on the job front.

The rental property was for a short time nice to live in until more problems began to surface. The first few weeks had been rough going but with the initial water quality problem solved we enjoyed a few weeks of problem free living along with plenty of nice hot showers and baths for the children! Alas the comfort, peace and tranquillity of country living were again to be shattered. I have never in my life lived in a rental property with so many problems and it was all getting a bit tiresome and tedious.

It was the Canada Day bank holiday weekend with Canada Day itself falling on the Sunday. Regina holds an annual festival with all sorts of different activities and many stalls to keep people of all walks of life amused and as night falls the piece de résistance is usually a huge spectacular fireworks display. It was to be our first Canada Day so we planned to go along with most of the population of Regina and have a good time. Well the day before the Canada Day celebrations our electronic garage door had its owns plans for us and decided to jam itself shut so that there was no way we could get the car out. It certainly appeared that our first Canada Day was to be spent sat in the house twiddling our thumbs! Thankfully the landlady managed to get her handyman over to have a look at the garage and he temporarily fixed it. The hinges had come adrift so the door had fallen at a silly angle and become jammed. After a few good bangs with a hammer and some brut force it was working efficiently enough for us to be able to open the door and get the car in and out. Every morning in that house we would wake up with that feeling of dread of what could go wrong next. It had become such a regular occurrence that it was expected and more often than not we would not be wrong in our prediction. Hopefully it would be an enjoyable disaster free Canada Day.

The garage door was just the beginning of a long period of some quite serious problems within the house. We had noticed a mouse in the garage some weeks before and thought it rather cute and harmless so we kindly treated it to some crackers. After a few days we came to realise that the little mouse along with its friends were not so cute when we discovered that they had been happily letting themselves into our house. The initial signs were mouse droppings in the house along the skirting boards and the rubbish had been chewed in the bin each morning under the sink. At first the problem did not seem too bad so we went out and purchased the usual mousetraps and placed them around the house. Within the first few hours of setting the traps with cheese four mice had been caught, we really had been invaded! They were obviously not shy and not bothered about the fact that I was sitting writing the manuscript for this book whilst they scurried around. Once a mouse had been caught we simply took the mouse off the trap and disposed of the body and disinfected the catch site. We had no idea at that time of the danger we were putting ourselves in.

Our next-door neighbour happened to call that first day of the mouse trouble saga and we were glad she did. We explained that we had some furry critters as lodgers and she told us that we had to clean up after them in a certain way due to the fact that deer mice can carry a harmful disease. The procedure was simple but until we knew what to do we had not followed it. The whole area including the dead mouse had to be engulfed with a strong disinfectant preferably bleach as the droppings and urine of the mice were potentially very bad. We went straight to the Internet and found that deer mice can carry a disease called Hantavirus that can be fatal to humans and although it is very rare it was a risk that we were not prepared to take, not with children. The disease is carried in airborne particles from the mouse's droppings and urine so when cleaning an area where mice have been we were told that it was advisable to wear a mask so it had to be taken very seriously. The landlady was informed and a local pest control company came out to the house and laid poison traps. Not a nice way to go but it had to be done. All that could be done had been done so it was a case of letting the poison slowly do it's work and hope that the problem would get better over the first few weeks of the poison bait being down.

On a good note we had some goods news regarding one of the jobs in Manitoba, the Medical Laboratory Technologist post Lance had applied for in Portage la Prairie. After speaking to the senior technologist it looked promising so we arranged to go over to Portage la Prairie to have a scout of the area and to give Lance the opportunity to have a look at his new potential place of work. We were both pleased with the outcome as we had done our homework on both places and found Portage to be the leading city. Lance had not heard back from the pharmaceutical company in Steinbach regarding the second position he had applied for but we had learnt to bide our time and just wait. Things in Canada just take a little while longer than we usually expect but Lance was finally contacted and a phone interview was arranged. The position in Steinbach was Lance's second choice even though it would have been a change to his eight years of hospital laboratory work and a new exciting diversion into the manufacturing of medicines.

The only downside to the position in Portage la Prairie was the poor annual leave entitlement but that is pretty much the same throughout the country in Lance's occupation. Whilst I am on the subject of annual leave in any employment situation, I would like to offer a small piece of advice. It is an idea to negotiate annual leave entitlement before accepting a position, asking the employer to take into consideration your years of practice and experience if any. That was very much a sore point, as we did not do that with the Regina job. Unfortunately once a job has been accepted it is too late and you have to get on with the notion of little if any annual leave for the first twelve months. Other occupations may have different annual leave entitlements but it is a very wise idea to ask first and if needed negotiate.

The interview day for the Steinbach position came and Lance had prepared himself as best as he could by reading up about the job requirements he was a little unsure about. With the position being a completely new area for him he was slightly out of his league in some areas but in other ways he fitted the job description well. Lance's telephone interview did not go well, in fact it was the worst interview Lance has ever had and it was clearly obvious that he had been unsuccessful in his application. The interview consisted of a panel of four people who literally raked him over the coals by asking him very difficult closed questions that he struggled to answer. He even admitted that it was that bad and stressful he could have quite easily put the phone down on them and forgotten the whole thing. Lance did his best as he always does but when a company wants the best of the best in that area and you do not have enough knowledge in that area then you have little hope. It looked very likely that we would be accepting the Portage la Prairie position and that was what we wanted.

The rentals water well had still not been shocked by that point in time and with the summer heat we were starting to notice a very strong egg odour and black bacteria growing in the toilets. That was a very clear indication that the water in the well needed to be treated promptly.

Before the procedure was done we had both joked about the iron corroded pipes and rusty old pump in the basement breaking into bits after the shocking solution had gone through the system. The day after the well had been treated we had to drain the water out of the well using a hosepipe until the chlorine smell was very slight. With all of that done it was time to turn the water softener back on. During the shocking process it had been turned onto bypass, as we did not want chlorine contaminated water going into the conditioning system. Everything appeared well and in good working order. The water was cleaner than ever and at last after two months of fairly bad water quality we were able to use nice clean water, for a few hours anyway!

That night we could not understand why the pump in the basement was continuously on as it should have only pumped water when water had been used or was in use in the house and at that time of night no water was being used. Toilets were checked in case they were leaking and taps double checked to the point that they were extra tight but the pump kept on pumping. Our joke was turning into a reality and it was about to get a whole lot worse. The next morning we went to have a look at the rusted heap of metal that was the water pump and noticed that it had a leak, a continuous leak. With a huge leak the pump was never going to stop so we phoned the landlady and she arranged for a plumber to come and have a look at it. That was on a Friday and it was a long bank holiday weekend so we hoped that the problem would be easily solved. Not to be, the whole pump was basically condemned and taken away. Leaving us with no running water to either wash with or more worrying to flush the toilet with.

Yet again Canada had dealt us another blow, well that is how we saw it any way. Since arriving everything had seemed to go the wrong way for us, it was all becoming a very hard struggle. Not for the first time since we had been in Canada we really did think of packing up at that point and with tails between legs returning to the UK. It was a real mental battle for us both but we knew if we could get past all of the troubles we were dealing with in Canada at that time it would eventually turn out to be a much better place to live. Going back to the UK would have been so much harder with trying to find a job and more importantly an affordable house to live in. It was a really close fight for a while but Canada won after we thought logically about the whole thing.

Since moving to the property at the beginning of June 2007 we had not drunk the water in the well opting like most people to buy eighteen litre bottles of water for drinking purposes. Buying extra to wash the dishes and wash ourselves did not seem too bad at first as we thought that the problem would be short lived, a day at the most! The plumber could not salvage the pump and there was nothing else he could do but replace it. Again unlucky for us as he did not know when he could replace it so one day without water was turning into possibly more than two days.

One toilet flush took nearly one full eighteen litre bottle and we soon found that we were going to the supermarket everyday to buy at least four eighteen litre bottles of pure filtered water to flush away! So with a big mouse problem and no means of sanitation things looked bleak for the Bairds. The plumber finally arrived with the new pump three days after he had initially took the old one away and turned all the water off. Things looked more positive for once and we hoped to have had full running water by the end of that day. You may be able to guess going on our run of bad luck that it was not to be. The pump was fitted and the water turned back on but the pump did not pump and it became clear that there was a greater problem elsewhere in the water works system. So with a new pump in place the situation was no better than the day the old one had been removed, three days prior to be exact! According to the plumber the problem was in the well and in order to rectify the problem he would have to drain the well and go into it to have a look. It was Sunday and with the long weekend he would not be able to find a helper until Tuesday, great another couple of days without water.

We were by then very fed up with the attitude of our landlady and we had been patronised enough regarding our obvious fault in her eyes of the problems in the property. She seemed to insinuate as each problem arose that we had in someway been the cause of the problem. The true fact was the house that she was actually trying to sell was a complete and utter horror house that had not been properly maintained or built in our eyes. That Sunday was the final straw for us. We had more than enough to cope with without the unnecessary e-mails from our so called caring landlady that was only caring about her bank balance from the sale of the house when it happened. We had to suggest after three days of after having no showers or baths that she paid for us to go to a hotel so we could have a proper wash. A decent landlord should have suggested alternative accommodation from the first day of having the water turned off but her true colours had been well and truly shown. She could not be bothered and was not in the slightest bit concerned for our welfare or health during such a risky time. We felt so annoyed that we actually took our issues to the rental ombudsman and to a local lawyer hoping in some way to make the landlady apologise for the treatment we had received. Again we realised that Canadian rules are not what we expected and it turned out that she was in some areas wrong. However she could actually write what she liked in the e-mails that she sent to us even if it was completely over the top and very hurtful. That was not good enough so we did proceed to inform her that we had taken legal advice and that if she carried on with silly accusations and her patronising attitude we would be left with no option but to take the matter further. In a way that small white lie did work for a short while and she did appear to be worried about our actions. She agreed to pay for a hotel room and reimburse us for the expense we had incurred and for the inconvenience we had endured.

The plumber had indeed found a helper and he arrived bright and early on the Tuesday morning to pump the well, five o'clock in the morning! Once the water had been emptied the problem was found quickly. The filter that the water went through was well and truly blocked so after a new filter was fitted the pump was turned on and it finally sprung into life. For some reason we thought we would have clean running water almost instantaneously but the well had been stirred up during the process of fitting the new filter so the water resembled a dark chocolate milkshake colour. Chocolate milkshake water was not acceptable. It was not the plumber's fault as he had fixed the problem but his time in the well had stirred all the sediment up and it would take three days or more for the water to clear and for it to be useable.

We took that as a good opportunity for us to go away for a few days and explore Portage la Prairie. One to see if it was a suitable place to move to and to have a look at the hospital where Lance could be working. We had not made a decision on the job at that point but from the interview and from what we could find out on the Internet it did not seem too bad a place at all. We arranged to view a few properties whilst we were there to give us an idea of what we could get for our money and we hoped that it would be a lot more than we could have got in Regina. Unfortunately we had moved to Saskatchewan about eight months too late, our usual trick of missing the boat and by the time we arrived house prices had literally sky rocketed. The cause of that increase was the huge influx of old Saskatchewan residents returning home from many money making years in Alberta to buy up the cheap property in many areas of Saskatchewan. Big spending power and greedy real estate agents saw the market increase rapidly and out of reach for many like us.

The idea of a nice big acreage was again thwarted. However since arriving in June 2007 we soon came to realise that big city living in any shape or form was not for us and buying a property in Regina, not that we could afford one was not what we wanted. We had come from a small town in Wales and our time in New Zealand was also spent in a small city so our thoughts of not settling in the big city of Regina had indeed been correct. We had to find a smaller place to live and sooner rather than later. The children had been out of school for quite a few months by then and although I was home schooling them some of that time it was important that they got back into the swing of the education system. It was also important for us as a family to find somewhere that we would be happy. The problems with the rental house and the Jekyll and Hyde landlady we had been in contact with over time had placed us in a very stressful situation. We found that the added stress was causing arguments and tension between us as a close family, and the underlying problem that Lance did not like his new job at all did not help at all. We needed to move and move fast, so we turned our attention to the small community of Portage la Prairie in central Manitoba.

Our first visit to Portage la Prairie was promising, the city was small and there was a good feeling about the place. I have to say that it is always a good idea to go on your first gut instinct as that first impression is usually right. We explored the area well and viewed some nice properties on the second day; it was all seeming to be falling into place.

Farewell Regina!

On returning back to Regina to face water that had not yet cleared, a nagging landlady from hell and a rather unfriendly city the decision to accept the job in Portage hospital came easy, very easy in fact.

I have to go back here briefly to our horrid water problem. I mentioned in the New Zealand section of this book the unbearable heat that we endured during the summer months spent positively roasting in Gisborne, well I would like to take that back in some ways! Our idea of becoming a spit roast in New Zealand took on a shallower theme once we experienced the scorching prairie heat in Regina. Some days the heat and the humidity made it feel like forty-five degrees and that was uncomfortable. Literally sitting motionless was a hard task and lack of sleep took on a whole new meaning. The lack of good water to wash with was a very big deal especially when we felt the need to shower more than once a day.

Now we shall go back to the original topic that started this section. Our prayers had been answered and the Bairds had once again found something to get their teeth into and that provided some well-needed motivation. We could finally start to look for a house to call home and finally arrange to receive our long awaited sixty-seven boxes of belongings that had been in storage in Vancouver for what seemed like months. In fact it was only one month at that time. Whilst in Portage la Prairie we did see two properties that interested us and we arranged to travel back to have another look. The journey from Regina to Portage la Prairie is around the five-hour mark, that's how long it takes us anyway. So for us to try and undertake a round trip in one day was not such a good idea.

Due to Lance's work commitments in the Regina General Hospital we had to arrange the next visit to be three weeks after the first. We hoped that in that time the properties we had viewed had not sold, as the other options were not too hot. We had been clever enough to arrange our mortgage in advance so our next trip would be to offer on one of the two properties. Our favourite was a small holding with six acres just ten minutes outside of the city. It was a good house, maybe a tad small but the land was useable for my dream of self-sufficiency and that was the places main selling point along of course with the quiet country setting. The other property was at the other end of the scale; a large four-bedroom family home with no acreage as such but the garden was a good size. The house was located on the outskirts of the city. Pricey buy but very nice and in a good neighbourhood.

The three weeks leading up to our second visit was spent mainly as usual, confirming mortgage details and hoping we would not miss out on the country small holding in the meantime. Those three weeks passed quickly and we were soon back in Portage la Prairie to face some disappointing news that the owners had indeed accepted an offer. We were not yet out of the running and after viewing the four-bedroom home again we decided to counter offer on the country house. Our problem was Lance had arranged to start work the first week of October 2007 so our possession date would have to be four weeks from the date we had our offer accepted. To cut a long-winded story short the old couple in the house had not found a new house to move into so it was unlikely that they would accept our higher counter offer due to the short possession date we needed. Our fears were met and they refused. They were elderly and did not want to move into temporary accommodation and then into a new house within a short space of time plus they felt obliged to the initial couple that had offered first. A lesser amount but they had stipulated a longer possession date. The good life was not to be, again. I had really hoped that it would be ours, but the other offer came three days before we arrived in Portage la Prairie. Beaten to it by three days, Can you believe it? Those country sufficiency books would be left to gather dust on the shelves for a few years more, nevermind.

Despite our obvious disappointment that we had missed out on our first choice we were happy that our offer on the four-bedroom home was accepted. If you can imagine an English barn conversion cross a Swiss chalet you will have a reasonably good idea of what our new house looks like. We were happy to get it but also slightly apprehensive about the pending costs of living in such a nice home. We had struggled in New Zealand with the living costs of owning a nice home and the house in Portage la Prairie was another step up again so with Lance on similar wages in comparison to New Zealand it was understandable to why we did have concerns.

Lance's wages would be increased once he passed the Canadian Society for Medical Laboratory Science exam. Failing would be expensive and if he could not pass that exam his job would be basically void. The job was in a way temporary until he passed the five-hour exam. The very strict exam that covers areas that he is not familiar with (at the time of writing anyway)

The pass mark for that exam sits at eighty percent so a very tall order for a laboratory technologist trained outside of Canada. It was yet again a huge gamble but we could not live in Regina so a gamble we had no option in taking.

With house and job definitely in the bag we set about the task of arranging the removal truck. Unlike the UK were the majority of people hire a company to move their belongings we opted to do the do it yourself version as many do over here in Canada. We hired a twenty-four foot removals van to be picked up the day prior to our move. Our move date at that time was actually not set as on the paperwork the possession date was to be the 1st October. However the sellers knowing that we wanted to get the children back into school suggested an earlier possession date might be possible. After a few false starts the possession date was finalised for the 25th September, a little earlier than first thought.

Not a problem to us at all, the sooner the better as far as we were concerned. We had just about had enough of the rental and the landlady so we were more than happy to tell her we were moving out and happy to let her know that we did not intend to let her know where we were going to. We certainly did not want to have any further dealings with her. In a way it was sad that she turned out to be that way, over the years we had spent working on our Canadian Immigration we had been in touch with her on and off and she had been helpful. She had supposedly done that as a friend but as soon as she realised we did not intend to buy a house through her in Regina she changed. I cannot generalise on all real estate agents but I can say that some are definitely only in it for their benefit and they think little of the clients they pretend to want to help. They are only interested in the money you have available to spend and work to their best ability to get you to cough up more than you intend to spend! Despite our views we had been given a chance to start a life in Canada properly and we intended to give it our all to make it work.

The final weeks spent in Regina were exiting. We had a big new house to fill with stuff and although we did have our New Zealand belongings coming the decorative knick knack side of things were scarce so we spent a small amount of money in the local stores buying some well needed furniture, appliances and knick knacks to put around our new home.

We had been in Regina since June 2007 and we were surprised on the amount of stuff that we had accumulated in the three and a half months we had been there. You know the type of stuff I mean, those items that get shoved in the cupboards and forgotten about, those items that fall out on top of you when you open it! Well we had quite a few boxes to fill with those miscellaneous cupboard collections and the rental was filling up nicely with packed boxes and our new items. To be honest we actually thought a twenty-four foot truck would be too small but it turned out that they had messed up our booking anyway and we were allocated a twenty-six foot truck instead.

Lance had seen enough of the hospital in Regina, the stupid rules, the non existent training and the not so friendly staff so he decided with all the packing and finalities to be done he would finish his job earlier than he had anticipated. That was fine by me as I was a packer, a cleaner, a full time homemaker and anything else that was asked of me in-between so I was not ashamed to say the extra help was more than welcome.

On the 24th September 2007 we packed up our huge moving truck with our belongings. We said our farewells to the less than appealing rental and headed out of Regina for the five-hour journey to our new home in Portage la Prairie, Manitoba. It is also here that I am going to end our journey, for now anyway. I am certain that I will feel the need to indeed put pen to paper or rather fingers to keyboard in the future and share with you our story once again as I am sure we will encounter further ups and downs along the way.

I hope that all who have felt our heartaches, happiness and joy will look forward to revisiting the Bairds someday soon, Did Lance pass his exam? Did we settle in Portage la Prairie, Manitoba and the big question after all our hard work over the last few years, Was Canada what we thought it would be and a country to call home? Thank you to all of you who have shared your time with us, we all hope you will join us again one day.

Afterword

Firstly I would like to say that I hope you have enjoyed sharing the Baird family emigration experience, we have enjoyed bringing the book to you.

My intentions for writing were to bring to you the reader a true insight into the process of moving from your home country through the eyes of a family of five. To bring forward our times of anguish, sorrow and indeed joy in order to put together a true picture of how it is possible to succeed in finding a new start.

It may appear that some of our time spent away travelling was not worth the hassle, namely New Zealand and I can understand the logic behind those thoughts. Yes it was hard and the New Zealand part of this book does appear to be nothing but doom and gloom. Our mistake was the fact that we did not research our destination in New Zealand thoroughly enough. We took the first job that came about and leapt in with both feet without really thinking it through. Time was not on our side but that is no excuse. However on the other side of the coin we did have some fabulous times in Gisborne, New Zealand. We met some great people and we travelled to some wonderful places. Gisborne was not what we assumed it to be on first appearance from the information that we gathered on the Internet prior to moving there but for eighteen months it was our home and we are thankful for the experience and the time that we spent in that small North Island city.

Emigration is the new twentieth century phenomenon that is increasing not just in the UK but also in many other countries around the world. Many of us will never emigrate but if we are honest with ourselves most of us will have a small part of curiosity about this new intriguing phenomenon that has grabbed the world somewhere inside of us. After all it is human nature to wonder and dream.

I hope that this book has given you that curious insight and made you smile. For those who have read this book and intend to or already have emigrated I hope that you enjoyed our experiences. There are many to follow in our footsteps and I wish you all the luck in the world. Your hard work and diligence will hopefully work for you as it did for us, believe in your dreams.

Emigration can sometimes feel like a very lonely experience. I must admit when we were thinking of emigrating and going through the different stages I would have liked to have been able to relate and share in depth what we were going through with others. Unfortunately there are not too many true-life books out there to read. Yes you can get the general books that concentrate on a particular country, and although they provide beneficial information they cannot provide heartfelt experiences.

These past few years we have worked hard, laughed hard and cried hard but despite all of that we would not turn the clock back. It is true to say that in hindsight we would have done some things differently but that is all part and parcel of the adventure.

Emigration is a wonderful experience providing that research and planning thoroughly is high on the agenda. We followed those simple rules and successfully accomplished our end goal and we were finally after all the ups and downs rewarded with a fantastic new life.

Resources

I have listed a few web addresses here that may be of help or of interest to you. Please be aware that at the time of writing these websites were valid. However they are subject to change at any time.

My website address

www.em-migrate.com

Immigration

Citizenship and Immigration Canada
www.cic.gc.ca

Immigration New Zealand
www.imigration.govt.nz

Useful Immigration Sources

www.emigrate2.co.uk
www.visalaw.com

Employment

www.monster.com
www.workopolis.com
www.jobs-emplois.gc.ca (Canada)

www.healthstaffspecialists.com (New Zealand)
www.moh.govt.nz/districthealthboards (New Zealand)

Holiday Accommodations

www.wcmcampers.com (Canada)
www.apollo.com (Australia)
www.williamsonlakecampground.com
Highly recommended site in Revelstoke, British Columbia

Brookside Motels, 36 Cox Street, Geraldine
www.accommodationnz.co.nz/geraldine-accommodation.shtml

Money Broker

www.hifx.com
This is the company we used on both occasions to transfer our funds

978-0-595-48513-0
0-595-48513-8

Manufactured by Amazon.ca
Bolton, ON

38509704R00122